Child Support

Through small group counseling

by Lois Landy

CHILD SUPPORT
Through Small Group Counseling

Copyright © 1990, KIDSRIGHTS, revisions and illustrations
Copyright © 1984, Lois Landy, original text

Resources updated 2002

Published by **KIDSRIGHTS®** a division of Jist Life, LLC
8902 Otis Avenue
Indianapolis, IN 46216
800-892-5437
fax: 877-543-7001
www.jistlife.com

12   11

Printed in the United States of America

ISBN 1-55864-005-3

This book is dedicated to my son, Bobby -
a young fellow who encourages me to look at life
as if I'm seeing it for the first time.

TABLE OF CONTENTS

The purpose of this book is to provide the busy counselor of young people with a quick reference for small group work. It is not intended to be a comprehensive solution to all the difficulties which the child from ages 6 to 12 experiences. It is intended to offer some structure and activities based on experience from which a counselor or teacher might draw and expand in order to create a program satisfying to one's own situation. It is also intended to provide some motivation to that professional who has been intending to do some group work, but for whatever reasons, has not yet begun.

This book represents a starting block of support for the counselor/teacher who is interested in becoming involved in small group counseling. My wish for those using this book is that each experience with small group counseling leads to some personal growth within the adult as well as the children, for it is that growth which will serve as a catalyst for continued involvement.

Lois Landy

Developmental counseling for students ages 6 to 12 is the process of designing guidance activities and programs to satisfy particular needs of children which appear as they develop and grow. Such needs may be the result of voids in a child's early years, a lack of exposure to appropriate role models, or a lack of readiness on the part of the child to master the personal or social development skills. Such needs may be identified by astute adults in the child's life in the course of daily interaction or they may surface in time of emotional crisis. Either way, what is important is that the counselor/teacher/parent attempt to help the child through the development of needed skills in a methodical, organized way. Appropriate exposure, interaction, and experiences are key ingredients which can help to encourage such development. Small group counseling is an ideal setting for this development to begin. The units in this guide are organized for an appropriate length of time to <u>begin</u> the development. Additional group time or teacher/parent follow-through is very important to encourage further development.

ORGANIZATION OF GROUPS

Counseling groups may be organized in countless ways. This counselor makes a plea to teachers, parents, and administrators in the early part of the school year and then again, at about mid-year, for prospective referrals for the various groups. It should be pointed out that referral is an on-going process. Appropriate referrals are accepted all year long. Students frequently refer themselves. The person making the referral is asked to identify some student behavior for which the child may need counseling services. The counselor usually discusses this input with the referrer, assigns students to groups according to an area of development, and sets up a schedule of meeting times. Groups meet weekly for periods of 30-60 minutes, depending on the age of the students, the purpose of the group, and the schedules of the children. Specifics are listed in the following units. On the day of each group meeting, this counselor places a note in the teacher's mailbox, notifying the student of his meeting time. Examples of these notes follow:

Student's Name _____   Teacher _____

                                            Date _____

I am looking forward to meeting with you today at _____

                                            Counselor _____

Student's Name _____   Teacher _____

Our group will meet today at _____

Date _____   Counselor _____

Group meetings should be cancelled only under dire circumstances. It is <u>very important</u> that students know their sessions will be held regularly at specified times. Dependability on the part of the counselor goes a long way toward building trust.

There will be <u>occasional</u> times when a counselor will have to postpone or cancel sessions. The following notes can be used as a way of notifying the students.

Student's Name _____   Teacher _____

Date _____

    Our group meeting must be rescheduled this week to _____
    Date

at _____ I'm looking forward to seeing you then.
    Time

Counselor _____

Student's Name _____   Teacher _____

Date _____

I am sorry our group will not meet this week as planned. I'll see you next week at our regular time.

Counselor _____

MAKE-UP OF THE GROUPS

As mentioned earlier, the groups are made up of students who share similar concerns. They may be children of the same sex, but this is not likely to happen often. They may all come from one class or they may come from several classes. They may all be from the same grade level or they may be from two or three grade levels. Generally, the groups are made up of 6-10 students.

PARENTAL PERMISSION FOR GROUP PARTICIPATION

Once a student is invited to join a guidance group, this counselor sends a letter home to the parents, informing them of the purpose and procedure for such participation. Inquiries from parents are invited. A parental signature acknowledging receipt of the letter is requested.

Parental permission is requested for participation in the Alcohol, Divorce, Death, and Incarceration groups prior to the first meeting. A counselor may desire permission for participation in other groups too, depending on the situation.

A sample of a parent letter can be found in Appendix A of this guide.

INTRODUCTORY GROUP SESSION

The first time the group assembles is a critically important time. At this meeting, the counselor sets the stage for future meetings. The counselor must be warm and reassuring yet firm. The appropriate procedures for entering the room, for waiting for the counselor if she is busy, for interacting with other group members, etc. are discussed. Ground rules and expectations are set.

This counselor insists upon group adherence to the policy: Nothing that will intentionally hurt another person in the group will be tolerated. This eliminates verbal put-downs and physical confrontations. This is not intended to eliminate healthy discussions between members who have disagreements. Appropriate verbal confrontations which can be channeled and controlled are encouraged as an important skill for students to develop.

At this first group meeting and every meeting which follows, the counselor and the students initiate the session with the <u>Name Game</u> activity. It is a simple procedure whereby the first person says, "My name is _____. What is your name?" as she turns to the person on her left. That person says, "My name is _____. Her name is _____. What is your name?" as he turns to the person on his left. And so it goes around the circle.

Repeating this activity every session accomplishes a couple of purposes.

1. It reviews the names of the children for the counselor and for the other group members who might only have contact with each other during the group sessions.
2. It signals the beginning of the session and sets somewhat of a serious tone.

Following the Name Game, the counselor introduces the <u>Group Discussion</u> time. Each group member has an opportunity to verbalize his thoughts/feelings on the topic. Each group member has the privilege of "passing" with no questions asked if he so desires.

Following the Group Discussion Time, the counselor asks if anyone has anything he would like to share with the group. The members have the opportunity to respond, offer suggestions, share similar situations, discuss a personal problem, etc. Confidentiality as a responsibility of each group member is discussed at the very first meeting and is inherent in each and every meeting thereafter.

On a given day, the group members' sharing time may consume all of the group session. The group session should be organized with enough flexibility so as to meet the needs of the group members. With much discussion and interaction, there may be no need or time for any additional activity. On most days, however, the group will be ready to participate in further activity. The units which follow include such therapeutic activities in a sequential manner so as to provide the students with a variety of meaningful experiences. There is no rule which says a group must complete all of the activities in each session, nor is a group restricted to a specified number of sessions. Again, flexibility in organizing and scheduling is the privilege and responsibility of the counselor.

At the initial group meeting, this counselor asks or helps each child to complete a self-concept survey (see Appendix B) and an incomplete sentences work sheet (see Appendix C). Students are asked to decorate an individual folder with pictures or words which tell something about themselves. The students' inventories and work sheets are filed in the folders in the counselor's office. Any additional paper work activities are added to it. At the end of the sessions the students receive their folders to take home.

Also at the initial group meeting, the counselor explains the purpose of the group and the procedures through which the students are referred. If time allows, <u>Goal Setting</u> takes place next. Goal Setting may also be planned for a second meeting if necessary. The importance of goal setting cannot be stressed enough. The goals may be written down on one chart for the entire group or each student may be asked to make a chart with the group goals as well as a few individual goals.

At the end of each group session the counselor asks individuals if they feel they have worked toward the goals of the group during that session. The counselor also asks the group members if the individual has done so. There must be a consensus that a person has cooperated and contributed to the group in order for that person to mark his success card with a smiley face.

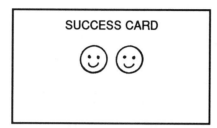

Students who are disruptive or indifferent may not mark their cards. In the event of disagreement over the student's eligibility for a smiley face, the counselor has the final say. This <u>Evaluation</u> activity concludes each session. The counselor may extend it further by setting five smiley faces as a goal for a special reward (pencil, eraser, note pad, discount ticket for a hamburger, etc.).

At the conclusion of the last session, the group members are asked to evaluate the group meetings. A sample of this evaluation form is included in Appendix D.

In summary, the initial session(s) include the Name Game, Group Discussion Time (structured and unstructured), Self-Concept Inventory, Incomplete Sentences Work Sheet, Review of Guidelines, Goal Setting, Preparation of Folders, and Evaluation. Each session which follows continues to include the Name Game, Group Discussion Time, and Evaluation. The outlines which follow should actually begin during the second meeting with the students.

Anger &
Aggression
Group

OBJECTIVES

1. To identify anger as a normal, healthy emotion experienced by everyone.
2. To identify the kinds of situations which generally provoke anger in one's self and how one typically deals with it.
3. To understand that there are appropriate and inappropriate ways of dealing with anger.
4. To identify the consequences which follow the inappropriate expression of anger in a school or home setting.
5. To practice alternative appropriate ways of expressing anger which do not hurt anyone or anything.

Target Group

Ages 6 to 8 and 9 to 12; 6-8 children per group.

Time Requirement

45 minutes per session; 7 sessions.

Whenever you see Name Game, it means:

A simple procedure whereby the first person says, "My name is _____. What is your name?" as she turns to the person on her left. That person says, "My name is _____. Her name is _____. What is your name?" as he turns to the person on his left. And so it goes around the circle.

Whenever you see Evaluation, it means:

At the end of each group session the counselor asks individuals if they feel they have worked toward the goals of the group during that session. The counselor also asks the group members if the individual has done so. There must be a consensus that a person has cooperated and contributed to the group in order for that person to mark his success card with a smiley face.

Students who are disruptive or indifferent may not mark their cards. In the event of a disagreement over the student's eligibility for a smiley face, the counselor has the final say.

This Evaluation activity concludes each session. The counselor may extend it further by setting five smiley faces as a goal for a special reward (pencil, eraser, note pad, discount ticket for a hamburger, etc.)

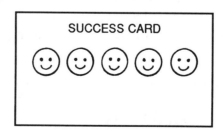

9

SESSION 1

Name Game

Group Discussion

You can tell if I'm angry by...

The group will view any appropriate video about anger and then discuss the film's message.

Materials

Construction paper   Writing paper
Plain white paper   Pencils

Directions

The counselor distributes ANGER NOTEBOOKS to each student.

The anger booklets are made up of two pieces of construction paper with the six pages shown above stapled in between.

Each student is asked to make a list of all the things or situations which make him angry, on page two of his booklet. Younger students may do it with pictures.

Homework

Ages 9 to 12

Each child selects from among available books on anger. His task is to read the book and share its message with the group at next week's meeting. He should pay particular attention to how the character handled his anger and at least one thing the book caused him to think about.

Some appropriate titles might include:

Alexander, Martha. *And My Mean Old Mother Will Be Sorry, Blackboard Bear*.

Conaway, J. *I'll Get Even*.

Hitte, K. *Boy Was I Mad!*

Marshall, J. *Miss Nelson Is Missing*.

Simon, N. *I Was So Mad*.

Viorst, J. *Alexander and the Terrible, Horrible, No Good, Very Bad Day*.

Watson, J., Switzer, R. & Hirschberg, J. *Sometimes I Get Angry*.

Evaluation

NOTES:

SESSION 2

Name Game

Group Discussion

The most anger I have ever felt.

Materials

Watson, J., Switzer, R., & Hirschberg, J. *Sometimes I Get Angry*.

Directions

Ages 6 to 8: The counselor reads *Sometimes I Get Angry* or another appropriate story to the group. Discuss.

Ages 9 to 12: The group members share what they experienced through their homework readings.

Conclude that there are many ways of handling anger. Some are appropriate and some are not appropriate.

Distribute ANGER BOOKLETS.

On the third page, each student is to list or draw the ways he usually expresses his anger.

Share with the group.

The counselor defines an appropriate way of handling anger as one which doesn't hurt anyone or anything. Each group member should go back through his list and underline all of the appropriate methods he uses. Compare the numbers of appropriate and inappropriate methods.

Homework

None.

Evaluation

NOTES:

SESSION 3

Name Game

Group Discussion

A time when I took my anger out on someone who didn't do anything to cause it.

Materials

Bubble Gum   Softee Bats
Old Pillows   Pound 'n Hollers

Directions

Distribute ANGER BOOKLETS.

Review some of the inappropriate ways of dealing with anger, for example, hitting someone.

Discuss the reaction to such a method.

Does the target of the anger hit back?
Does your teacher get angry with you?
Do you get sent to the principal? To your room?

The counselor points out that expressing one's anger inappropriately usually generates more anger.

The counselor explains that group members will have the opportunity to do some Madness Management Activities which are designed to release anger without hurting anyone or anything. Following the activities, the students will take time to record the exercises with words or pictures in their booklets (page four) under the heading: Appropriate Ways To Express Anger.

EXERCISE #1 Bubble Trouble

Each student receives a piece of bubble gum. He pretends the gum is the source of his anger. Upon the start signal, he begins chewing, first slowly and then faster and faster. He blows bubbles and pops them. Until the time limit (1-2 minutes) is up, he tries to "chew" the anger out of his bubble gum.

EXERCISE #2 Push It!

The students position themselves against an outside wall of the school. They pretend that the wall is the source of their anger. On signal, they push their hands, arms, shoulders, back, etc. against the wall. They push as hard as they can for 1 full minute.

EXERCISE #3 Beat It!

Taking an old pillow, each student beats with his fists on the pillow in an attempt to beat his anger out of his system. It's advisable for the students to cradle the pillow in their laps while beating to avoid hand injuries which might occur if the pillow is resting on a hard surface such as a floor or table. As an alternative, Softee Bats or Pound 'n Holler equipment may be used. Time limit: 1 minute.

EXERCISE #4 The Running Rage

Move outdoors to a track or gym field for this activity. The students imagine that the source of their anger is just ahead of them. The students begin to run after that "source". They start slowly and then begin to pick up the pace, until they are running as fast as they can. This activity can be adapted to running in place in which case a one minute time limit might be imposed.

EXERCISE #5 Glaring Glimpses

Position the students across from each other in twos. Have students on one side make faces ("cut eyes") at the other group. The second group then has permission to glare, sneer, growl, etc. back at their partners. No physical contact is allowed. Time limit: 1 minute per side.

Homework

None.

Evaluation

NOTES:

SESSION 4

Name Game

Group Discussion

A time when I suffered the consequences for getting angry.

Materials

Crackers	Finger painting paper or white shelf paper
Magazines	Finger paint

Directions

More Madness Management Activities:

EXERCISE #6 The Cracker Crunch

Students are to pretend that the soda crackers in the center of the table are the source of their anger. They begin munching slowly on the crackers, then munching faster as their anger intensifies. Time limit: 1 minute.

EXERCISE #7 Magazine Madness

Using old magazines, each student begins tearing up a magazine. He can tear single pages or several pages at a time. He must pretend that his anger is centered in the magazine pages. When time is called, the floor will be covered with a mound of paper. Students usually enjoy stuffing the scraps in the trash basket as another anger activity.

EXERCISE #8 Finger Painting Frenzy

Each student receives a sheet of finger painting paper (or glazed shelf paper) and a blob of finger paint. The student smears the paint over the whole paper and then draws objects of his anger. With one swish of his hand, he can "wipe out" his anger, redraw it, and wipe it out again.

The students record their activities in their ANGER BOOKLETS.

The counselor generalizes that the release of physical energy results in a release of emotional anger.

The students discuss their experiences with the activities.

Homework

None.

SESSION 4 continued

<u>Evaluation</u>

<u>NOTES:</u>

SESSION 5

Name Game

Group Discussion

A time I controlled my anger...

Materials

Newspapers   Paintbrushes
Movable eyes   Smooth rock for each student
Paint   Glue

Directions

Use a newspaper to discuss accidents or crimes which might have occurred as a result of uncontrolled anger. Discuss the importance of trying to control one's anger. Re-emphasize the need for a physical release of anger as a means of dispelling anger before it might be handled through talking things out.

Another Madness Management Activity.

EXERCISE #9 Angry Stone

Each student will paint a smooth rock, glue movable eyes on it, and paint an angry expression for its mouth. When the rocks have dried, the students will pretend to be angry. They will squeeze their rocks in their hands as hard as they can, allowing their anger to move through their arms into their stones. The students may take their angry stones home.

The students record the activity in their ANGER BOOKLETS.

Homework

None.

Evaluation

NOTES:

SESSION 6

Name Game

Group Discussion

Something that I've been angry about for a long time...

Materials

Spoon
Large mixing bowl
Measuring cup & spoons
Cookie tray
Waxed paper

Ingredients:
   3 cups oatmeal
   1½ cups brown sugar
   1½ cups flour
   1½ cups butter
   1½ teaspoons baking powder

Directions

Today the group will be making MADNESS MUNCHIES. WASH HANDS FIRST!

Group members should work together measuring and combining ingredients in a large bowl. Then they may take turns mixing the dough with their hands. The dough can be sectioned and distributed to the students. On waxed paper each group member can pound, knead, and mash the dough. The more anger that can be conjured up, the better mixed the dough will be. Bake on cookie tray for 10-12 minutes at 350°.

While cookies are baking, the counselor will direct the group through a series of relaxation exercises. The counselor will instruct the group to tense individual body parts and then relax. Some body parts to focus on include feet, knees, shoulders, elbows, hands, stomach, jaw, etc. To add to the calming atmosphere, soft music may be played.

Following the exercises, the group will discuss the importance of releasing angry feelings in an appropriate way and attempt to relax oneself before dealing with unresolved angry feelings.

Homework

None.

Evaluation

NOTES:

SESSION 7

Name Game

Group Discussion

I can tell I'm growing up emotionally because...

Materials

Finger puppets

Directions

Another <u>Madness Management Activity</u>.

EXERCISE #10   The Mad Monologue

Think about a person with whom you are angry. Imagine that person is the puppet on your hand. Tell the person what you are angry about. You may yell, move around, point your finger, shake the puppet; use a lot of energy. Continue for 1 minute.

Discuss the importance of verbalizing angry feelings. Discuss the significance of being able to <u>talk</u> about how you feel after you have worked through some of your anger in an appropriate way.

Record this activity in the ANGER BOOKLETS.

The students take turns <u>role playing</u> the situations which follow:

1. You have just returned home from school and discover your baby brother has gotten into your room. He has your things all over your room.

2. Your dad promised to give you money for the uniform you need by Saturday. The coach says you can't play without a uniform. Your dad comes home today and says he's sorry but he just won't have the money to give you this week after all.

3. The teacher leaves the room. You work quietly while she's gone, but David, who is in charge, writes your name down for talking. When the teacher returns, she tells you to stay after school for talking.

4. JoAnn is in your class. She is a troublemaker and you try to stay away from her, but out on the playground, she starts calling your mother names.

Allow the students to make up their own role plays using relevant situations.

SESSION 7 continued

Discuss the fact that controlling one's anger is not always an easy task but it is everyone's responsibility.

Homework

None.

Evaluation

NOTES:

ADDITIONAL RESOURCES

Books

Alexander, Martha. *And My Mean Old Mother Will Be Sorry, Blackboard Bear.*

Conaway, J. *I'll Get Even.*

Hitte, K. *Boy Was I Mad!*

Marshall, J. *Miss Nelson Is Missing.*

Simon, N. *I Was So Mad.*

Viorst, Judith. *Alexander and the Terrible, Horrible, No Good, Very Bad Day.*

Watson, J., Switzer, R., & Hirschberg, J. *Sometimes I Get Angry.*

Other Materials

Pound 'n Hollers

Softee Bats

Children of Alcoholism Group

OBJECTIVES

1. To study alcoholism as a disease.
2. To discuss the impact alcoholism has on the family.
3. To recognize and express one's feelings.
4. To learn that other students experience similar difficulties with alcohol in their families.
5. To identify the sources of help for the drinker and the drinker's family.
6. To identify coping strategies which children of alcoholics can use.
7. To practice decision making skills.

It is recommended that parental permission be secured for participation in this group.

Target Group

Ages 6 to 12; 6-10 students per group.

Time Requirement

45 minutes per session; 11 sessions.

Whenever you see Name Game, it means:

A simple procedure whereby the first person says, "My name is _____. What is your name?" as she turns to the person on her left. That person says, "My name is _____. Her name is _____. What is your name?" as he turns to the person on his left. And so it goes around the circle.

Whenever you see Evaluation, it means:

At the end of each group session the counselor asks individuals if they feel they have worked toward the goals of the group during that session. The counselor also asks the group members if the individual has done so. There must be a consensus that a person has cooperated and contributed to the group in order for that person to mark his success card with a smiley face.

Students who are disruptive or indifferent may not mark their cards. In the event of a disagreement over the student's eligibility for a smiley face, the counselor has the final say.

This Evaluation activity concludes each session. The counselor may extend it further by setting five smiley faces as a goal for a special reward (pencil, eraser, note pad, discount ticket for a hamburger, etc.)

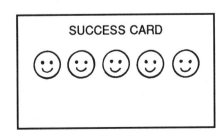

SESSION 1

Name Game

Group Discussion

Something I like other people to know about me.

Materials

None.

Directions

The counselor mentions the word DISEASE. Students respond with what comes to mind.

Next, the counselor mentions the word CANCER. This time, the counselor records on a chart the responses which come to the group members' minds.

Lastly, the counselor mentions the word ALCOHOLISM. Again, the counselor records the responses.

The counselor then asks the students to look at the two lists of words she's written. Are there any similarities or differences?

Discuss the idea that CANCER frequently evokes more empathy and understanding from others while ALCOHOLISM is frequently seen as something that could have been helped; that someone is to blame for being an alcoholic.

Emphasize that ALCOHOLISM is a disease just as CANCER is. Explain that an <u>alcoholic</u> is a person who has the disease of alcoholism. Stress the commonalities of suffering, treatment, etc.

Ask the children to share their experiences with ALCOHOLISM (verbally or with drawings).

Evaluation

NOTES:

SESSION 2

Name Game

Group Discussion

A feeling word that describes me is...

Materials

Index cards   String
Fabric crayons   Iron
Cloth banners   White Paper
Dowel rods

Directions

Given index cards, the students are asked to write down as many feeling words as they can think of which describe how they feel about the person in their lives who has a drinking problem. Stress honesty in identifying their feelings.

The counselor invites the group members to share their lists and to feel free to add words to or delete words from their lists as they listen.

Emphasize that it's OK to have negative feelings toward the person who has a drinking problem. Explain that, at times, mixed feelings are normal, too.

As a reminder of this, the students will decorate FEELINGS BANNERS. The counselor will already have cut fabric into a square and sewed a hem through which a dowel rod may be put and then tied with a string.

Using fabric crayons, the student decorates white paper, showing a feeling or several feelings they've experienced with regard to alcoholism. Using an iron, transfer the drawing from the paper onto the banner. Share the completed banners with the group.

Evaluation

NOTES:

SESSION 3

Name Game

Group Discussion

A time this past week when I experienced mixed emotions.

Materials

None.

Directions

The counselor presents the information:

ALCOHOLICS ARE <u>ADDICTED</u> TO ALCOHOL. That means once they start drinking, they cannot stop.

Discuss the questions:

What are some things you feel you could not live without?

What are some things other than alcohol that people are addicted to? (cigarettes, chocolate, caffeine, etc.)

Are all of these things harmful?

What are some things you've seen people do under the influence of alcohol which they may not have done if they'd been sober?

Explain that when a person drinks alcohol, it goes straight through the bloodstream to the brain. It does not have to be digested like food does. Because of this, alcohol affects behavior very quickly.

This would be an appropriate time to show a video on the physical effects of alcohol on the body.

Evaluation

NOTES:

SESSION 4

Name Game

**Group
Discussion**

Something I did once that I blamed on someone else.

Materials

Slips of White Paper

Directions

The counselor explains that ALCOHOLICS DO NOT ACCEPT RESPONSIBILITY FOR THEIR DRINKING. Sometimes they deny that they drink or say that it is someone else's fault.

What are some excuses you've heard people use?

Emphasize that NO ONE IS THE CAUSE OF SOMEONE ELSE'S DRINKING. Alcoholics drink because they have a disease called alcoholism.

BROKEN PROMISES

Ask each student to write one promise per slip of white paper which was made to him by the drinker. Encourage him to write as many promises as he can remember. When all of the children have finished writing, ask the students to tear in half any promise which was not kept. Talk about how it felt to have that promise broken.

Discuss the fact that drinkers frequently do not remember what they have promised.

Evaluation

NOTES:

SESSION 5

Name Game

Group Discussion

To me, alcoholism means...

Materials

None.

Directions

Invite a health professional to talk with the students about the physical effects of alcohol on the drinker.

Encourage questions from the students.

Some sample topics might include: drinking and driving; statistics on ages of drinkers; long term effects on memory, liver, etc.; effects on young drinker's growth; effects on unborn children.

Evaluation

NOTES:

SESSION 6

Name Game

Group Discussion

The person (people) in my life to whom I can talk about my problems is (are)...

Materials

Leite, E. & Espeland, P., *Different Like Me* or Shuker, N., *Everything You Need to Know About An Alcoholic Parent*

Directions

Distribute copies to each of the students. Encourage them to read it and share it with their families. If time permits, begin reading it together as a group.

The counselor emphasizes the need to talk with someone about worries and fears and to avoid holding everything inside.

Explain that there are sources of help available for the alcoholic and his family. Emphasize that an alcoholic must accept the fact that he needs help. It is his responsibility. Children can help by encouraging the alcoholic to seek help and reminding him that they still love him.

Ask the students to list as many sources of help as they can. Use the telephone book to look up phone numbers. Have the students record the numbers to take home with them.

Some treatment sources might include: hospitals, centers for the treatment of alcoholism, Alcoholics Anonymous (for the alcoholic), Al-Anon (for spouses of alcoholics), Alateen (for children of alcoholics).

Discuss the meetings held by the latter three groups.

Explain that Alateen is open to these students.

Evaluation

NOTES:

31

SESSION 7

Name Game

Group Discussion

A time I encountered a problem in my life for which I sought help.

Materials

None.

Directions

Invite a member of Alcoholics Anonymous, Al-Anon, and Alateen to visit with the group. Encourage any and all questions.

Some suggestions for the visitors might be:

1. Discuss how they recognize the problem in themselves or their family.
2. Discuss how the drinking problem has affected their lives.
3. What embarrassing moments, broken promises, fears, worries, etc. can be attributed to their experience with drinking?
4. Where and how did they seek help?
5. What advice would they offer these group members?
6. When and where do these group meetings take place?

Representatives from AA, Al-Anon and Alateen can provide free literature, some of which the counselor may feel is appropriate for the students.

Evaluation

NOTES:

SESSION 8

Name Game

Group Discussion

Open the group discussion time by soliciting comments or reactions to *Different Like Me* or *Everything You Need To Know About An Alcoholic Parent*.

Materials

Small, smooth rock for each student   Paint
Half sheet of 9 x 12 construction paper   Paintbrushes
Fine-line markers   Glue
Two movable eyes

Directions

Make a list of every way the students can think of to "cope" when the problem of drinking is making it a bad day at home.

Some suggestions might be:

1. Go to a friend's house.
2. Ride your bike.
3. Run.
4. Pick flowers.
5. Visit an elderly person in the neighborhood.
6. Go to your room.
7. Read a book.
8. Write a letter.
9. Exercise.
10. Do something nice for someone else.
11. Talk to someone you trust.
12. Color, paint, draw.
13. Write in a diary.
14. Sew.
15. Go for a walk.

Sitting around worrying or feeling sorry for oneself is not the answer. Getting "out of yourself", and getting involved with others is more constructive.

Discuss the difference between worries that we can control and those which we cannot control. Each student makes a WORRY WOCK and booklet.

Paint the rocks. When dry, glue two eyes on each. Fold the paper for booklet. Write message, whisper worry to the WORRY WOCK, and sign it.

(cover)
> If I can change that which worries me, I change it.
>
> If I cannot change that which worries me, I forget it and let the WORRY WOCK worry for me.

(inside)
> From this day forward, I hereby give my worries to the WORRY WOCK.
>
> Signed, _____

Evaluation

NOTES:

WORRY WOCK reprinted by permission of Bammie Cofield and Ann Spencer, Counselors, Ft. Benning Dependents School.

SESSION 9

Name Game

Group Discussion

One thing I did this past week to get my mind off my worries.

Materials

None.

Directions

Discuss the steps involved in the process of decision-making.

1. Identify the decision to be made.
2. Identify the choices (alternatives).
3. Consider the consequences of each alternative.
4. Decide which would be the best choice.
5. Make your decision.

Explain that statistics show that children of alcoholics are more likely to become alcoholics. Some medical studies show the possibility of an inherited tendency to become dependent on alcohol. These high-risk students must therefore become expert at making informed decisions about their own lives.

Use the following situation to work through the decision-making process as a group.

You've been left home alone. You wonder what is in your parents' liquor cabinet. You are curious about the taste of liquor.

What decision must be made?

What are your choices?

What are the probable consequences of each choice?

What is the best choice?

What is your choice?

Emphasize the reality of accepting consequences for one's choice.

Evaluation

SESSION 10

Name Game

**Group
Discussion**

A decision I've made for myself this past week.

Materials

None.

Directions

Allow each student to work through the decision-making process on his own for the following situation. It might be necessary to review the steps before they begin.

> Your friend, Nel, has invited you to her house. When you arrive you learn that her parents are gone for the day. Nel has invited several other kids too. Melanie, whom you have always thought of as a nice girl, surprises everyone by showing up with a bottle of wine. The others begin sipping it and making faces at its taste. They are giggling and seemingly having a lot of fun. They urge you to try it. They tease you by calling you "Sissy" and "Miss Goody Two Shoes" when you hesitate to join them. They do seem to be having a good time and you hate to be left out. On the other hand, you know if your parents found out, you'd be in big trouble. What will you do?

Share the answers with the group.

Discuss how peer pressure sometimes makes decision-making more difficult.

Evaluation

NOTES:

SESSION 11

Name Game

Group Discussion

Since we began this group to talk about alcoholism, I've learned...

Materials

Worksheet
Why Does Mom Drink So Much? video

Directions

Provide each student with the following work sheet.

> Pretend you are 14 years old.
> What could you do with $4.00 besides buy a six-pack of beer? List as many answers as you can.
>
> 1.
> 2.
> 3.
> 4.

Share the answers with the group. Discuss.

Entertain any questions the group might have about anything that's related to alcoholism.

Conclude by showing the video, *Why Does Mom Drink So Much?*

This video discusses what it is like to be a child of an alcoholic. It encourages children not to use that as an excuse for becoming less than what they are capable of becoming.

Evaluation

NOTES:

ADDITIONAL RESOURCES

Books

Black, Ph.D., C. *My Dad Loves Me. My Dad Has a Disease*.

Holland, R. *About Me*.

Leite, E. and Espeland, P. *Different Like Me*.

Rosenberg, M. *Not My Family*.

Shuker, N. *Everything You Need to Know About An Alcoholic Parent*.

Taylor, B. *Everything You Need to Know About Alcohol*.

Video

Why Does Mom Drink So Much? for pre-teens and older, 30 minutes.

Children of Incarcerated Parents Group

OBJECTIVES

1. To encourage open discussion about parents who are in prison.
2. To clarify and accept one's feelings about having a parent in prison.
3. To share concerns and situations which arise from being a child of an incarcerated parent.
4. To practice appropriate ways of expressing emotions.
5. To strengthen one's self-concept.

Target Group

Ages 6 to 12; 6-8 students per group.

Time Requirement

45 minutes per session; 6 sessions.

Whenever you see <u>Name Game</u>, it means:

A simple procedure whereby the first person says, "My name is _____. What is your name?" as she turns to the person on her left. That person says, "My name is _____. Her name is _____. What is your name?" as he turns to the person on his left. And so it goes around the circle.

Whenever you see <u>Evaluation</u>, it means:

At the end of each group session the counselor asks individuals if they feel they have worked toward the goals of the group during that session. The counselor also asks the group members if the individual has done so. There must be a consensus that a person has cooperated and contributed to the group in order for that person to mark his success card with a smiley face.

Students who are disruptive or indifferent may not mark their cards. In the event of a disagreement over the student's eligibility for a smiley face, the counselor has the final say.

This <u>Evaluation</u> activity concludes each session. The counselor may extend it further by setting five smiley faces as a goal for a special reward (pencil, eraser, note pad, discount ticket for a hamburger, etc.)

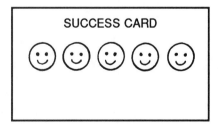

SESSION 1

Name Game

Group Discussion

If I had three wishes...

Materials

Burch, Robert. *Queenie Peavy*.

Directions

The counselor introduces *Queenie Peavy* - a story about a 13-year-old girl whose father is in prison. The counselor provides copies of the book to the students. If copies are not available or if the children are too young to read it, the counselor should have the story recorded on tape at a listening station. The group will read/listen to pages 5-40 together.

The group members are asked to tell ways in which Queenie and they are alike. Some similarities might be:

Parent in jail   Low economic status
Pretend they don't care   Good student
Poor attitude   Tells stories
In trouble at school   Has chores to do at home
Victims of teasing by peers   Feels the need to "get back"
                                                    at children who tease

Discuss what it's like to have a parent in prison and how each would like to change his situation if he could.

Homework

Read *Queenie Peavy* pages 41-82.

Evaluation

NOTES:

SESSION 2

Name Game

Group Discussion

A secret I have...

Materials

Burch, Robert. *Queenie Peavy*.
Construction Paper
Markers

Directions

The group reviews *Queenie Peavy* pages 41-82.

The group discusses the teasing Queenie endured.

List some feeling words which describe Queenie.

Discuss the teasing which upsets the group members.

List feeling words which describe the group members.

Each student will draw a picture of the person who is incarcerated in the center of a sheet of construction paper. Using markers, the students will fill the surrounding space with the feeling words which describe that person. Share with the group.

Homework

Read *Queenie Peavy* pages 83-108.

Evaluation

NOTES:

SESSION 3

Name Game

**Group
Discussion**

A feeling I have a difficult time expressing.

Materials

Burch, Robert. *Queenie Peavy*.	Large metal can
Writing paper	Matches
Pencils, pens, markers	

Directions

Discuss <u>anger</u> as an emotion.

Discuss how Queenie released her anger.

Discuss how each group member releases his anger.

Discuss various ways of releasing anger without hurting anyone or anything. Emphasize physical activities which release the energy of anger. (Refer to section on ANGER & AGGRESSION.)

ANGRY LETTER ACTIVITY

Each student writes a letter to someone who has angered him. In the letter he states exactly what has angered him. He may use any words to describe his anger because it will be up to the student to decide if he wishes to share it. It should be as long as he can make it, writing down every detail which has angered him. He may want to write with pencil, pen, marker, or whatever helps the emotion to flow.

Next, the student is given the option of sharing his letter (whole or part) or keeping it private. The group then wads their letters in an old metal can. They move outside where the counselor drops a lighted match into the can, allowing the letters to burn. If burning them is not feasible, tearing them into very small pieces and disposing of them in a trash can or dumpster will provide the same assurance that they are not being read by anyone else.

Discuss the necessity of "letting anger go". Discuss the unhealthy effect of harboring it inside oneself.

Homework

Read *Queenie Peavy* pages 109-138.

SESSION 3 continued

<u>Evaluation</u>

<u>NOTES:</u>

SESSION 4

Name Game

Group Discussion

If I were President of the United States...

Materials

Burch, Robert. *Queenie Peavy*	Two movable eyes
Small, smooth rock for each student	Paint
Half sheet of 9 x 12 construction paper	Paintbrushes
Fine-line markers	Glue

Directions

The group reviews *Queenie Peavy* pages 109-138.

Discuss worry as an emotion.

Discuss how Queenie handled her worry.

List the things Queenie worried about. List the things the students worry about.

With regard to the person who is incarcerated, discuss the worries of the group members.

The group makes WORRY WOCKS and booklets.

Directions

Paint the rocks. When dry, glue two eyes on each. Fold the paper for booklet. Write message below, whisper worry to the WORRY WOCK, and sign it.

> (cover)
> If I can change that which worries me, I change it.
>
> If I cannot change that which worries me, I forget it and let the WORRY WOCK worry for me.

> (inside)
>   From this day forward, I hereby give my worries to
>   the WORRY WOCK.
>
>   Signed, _____

Homework

Read *Queenie Peavy* pages 139-160.

Evaluation

NOTES:

WORRY WOCK reprinted by permission of Bammie Cofield and Ann Spencer, Counselors,
Ft. Benning Dependents School.

SESSION 5

Name Game

Group Discussion

Someone I'd like to get even with.

Materials

Burch, Robert. _Queenie Peavy_.   Glue
12 x 18 construction paper   Scissors
   for each student   Camera
Magazines   Markers

Directions

The group reviews _Queenie Peavy_ pages 139-160.

Discuss what Queenie could do that she could be proud of.

Identify some things each group member can be proud of.

Each group member makes a poster with words or pictures which depict those things of which he can be proud; something he can do...something he has...someone he knows...etc.

The counselor takes a picture of each child with an instant camera.

The students then paste their pictures on the posters.

The students label their posters: "I'm proud of..."

Homework

Read _Queenie Peavy_ pages 161-176.

Evaluation

NOTES:

SESSION 6

Name Game

Group Discussion

The best time of my life.

Materials

Burch, Robert. *Queenie Peavy.*

Directions

The group reviews *Queenie Peavy* pages 161-176.

The group identifies some of the things Queenie learned about her dad, her world, and herself.

Reflecting over the past five group sessions, the group members attempt to verbalize what each has learned using "I learned..." statements.

Discuss what each student thinks it must be like for the person who is incarcerated.

Discuss whether or not each student visits, calls, or writes the person who is incarcerated.

Allow the students time to draw a picture, write a letter or a story to that person. Offer to mail it from the school or allow the child to take it with him on his next visit.

Homework

None

Evaluation

NOTES:

ADDITIONAL RESOURCES

Books

Burch, Robert. _Queenie Peavy._

Cunningham, Carolyn. _All Kinds of Separation_.

Hickman, Martha. _When Andy's Father Went To Prison_.

Holland, R. _About Me_.

Death
Counseling
Group

OBJECTIVES

1. To provide students with facts regarding death and dying.
2. To explain death as a part of the cycle of life.
3. To provide the opportunity in a secure environment for students to ask questions and share experience about death.
4. To clarify and accept one's own feelings about death.

Target Group

Ages 6 to 8; 4-8 children per group.

Time Requirement

30 minutes per session; 6 sessions.

Target Group

Ages 9 to 12; 4-8 children per group.

Time Requirement

45 minutes per session; 7 sessions.

This group is designed for children who have experienced the death of a family member, friend, or pet.

Whenever you see Name Game, it means:

A simple procedure whereby the first person says, "My name is _____. What is your name?" as she turns to the person on her left. That person says, "My name is _____. Her name is _____. What is your name?" as he turns to the person on his left. And so it goes around the circle.

Whenever you see Evaluation, it means:

At the end of each group session the counselor asks individuals if they feel they have worked toward the goals of the group during that session. The counselor also asks the group members if the individual has done so. There must be a consensus that a person has cooperated and contributed to the group in order for that person to mark his success card with a smiley face.

Students who are disruptive or indifferent may not mark their cards. In the event of a disagreement over the student's eligibility for a smiley face, the counselor has the final say.

OBJECTIVES continued

This <u>Evaluation</u> activity concludes each session. The counselor may extend it further by setting five smiley faces as a goal for a special reward (pencil, eraser, note pad, discount ticket for a hamburger, etc.)

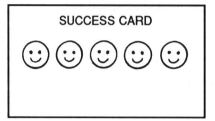

SESSION 1 Ages 6 to 8

Name Game

Group Discussion

Today I feel...

Materials

Index Cards
Pencils
Simon, Norma. *The Saddest Time*.

Directions

The group members make a Me Box on an index card.

My favorite person	My pet
How I look when I'm sad	Someone I knew who died

The group members share their Me Boxes.

The group members brainstorm how people die.

The counselor writes down their ideas.

Some suggestions might be:

age	murder
surgery	suicide
illness	execution
accident	

The counselor reads one story from *The Saddest Time* or any other appropriate story to the group. Discuss.

Evaluation

NOTES:

SESSION 2 Ages 6 to 8

Name Game

Group Discussion

The time my pet died.

Materials

Drawing paper   Crayons   Markers
Viorst, Judith. *The Tenth Good Thing About Barney.*

Directions

The counselor reads *The Tenth Good Thing About Barney,* a story about a child whose cat has died.

The students are asked to think about the person or pet in their lives who has died. They share what that special person left behind in the way of memories.

The students are asked to reflect on themselves and the fact that they will die someday because death is a natural part of life.

EPITAPHS ACTIVITY

On a piece of drawing paper, each child will draw a large headstone. On it, he will write his name and birth date. In pictures, each child will draw what he thinks people will remember about him.

Share tombstones with the group.

JOHN DAVIS
OCTOBER 22, 1974

Evaluation

NOTES:

SESSION 3 Ages 6 to 8

Name Game

Group Discussion

The time someone I loved died.

Materials

The Fall of Freddie the Leaf, video, 16 minutes.

Directions

The counselor explains briefly that everyone goes through certain stages when dealing with death. The counselor discusses denial, anger, bargaining, depression, and acceptance (Kubler-Ross).

The students view *The Fall of Freddie the Leaf* or another video on death.

Discuss how the characters in the video went through the five stages.

Each child is asked to relate from his own experience how he passed through any of the five stages in dealing with death.

Evaluation

NOTES:

SESSION 4 Ages 6 to 8

Name Game

Group Discussion

A time I came close to death!

Materials

Simon, Norma. *The Saddest Time*.
Puppets

Directions

The counselor reads another story from *The Saddest Time* or another appropriate story about death.

The students use puppets to play the parts of the characters of the story.

Given the following situations, the children <u>role play</u> the characters:

1. You are the one who must tell your 5-year-old sister that the family pet has been run over by a car.

2. Your best friend's older brother was killed in a motorcycle accident. What do you say to your friend?

3. Your teacher's mother died unexpectedly of a heart attack. Today is her first day back to school.

4. Your grandma is very sick and is not expected to live more than a week. Your mother asks if you would like to go visit her one last time.

Discuss how it felt to be the person affected by death or the person offering sympathy.

Evaluation

NOTES:

SESSION 5 Ages 6 to 8

Name Game

Group Discussion

When I see a friend of mine upset, I...

Materials

Drawing paper   Crayons
Markers   Fassler, Joan. *The Boy With a Problem*.

Directions

Provide students with paper and crayons or markers. Ask them to draw various ways people show their grief. Some possible ways might include: crying, being alone, becoming disinterested in school, hitting/striking out at others.

Try to get the group to label the various pictures with feeling words: sadness, anger, loneliness, guilt, hopelessness, worry.

Conclude the session by reading *The Boy With A Problem*, a story which explains how feelings are often hidden behind behaviors which don't fit the person's normal behavior.

Evaluation

NOTES:

SESSION 6 Ages 6 to 8

Name Game

Group Discussion

What worries me about dying.

Materials

Small, smooth rock for each student   Paint
Half sheet of 9 x 12 construction paper   Paintbrushes
Fine-line markers   Glue
Two movable eyes

Directions

Discuss the difference between worries that we can control and those which we cannot control. Each student makes a WORRY WOCK and booklet.

Paint the rocks. When dry, glue two eyes on each. Fold the paper for booklet. Write message written below, whisper worry to the WORRY WOCK, and sign it.

(cover)
   If I can change that which worries me, I change it.

   If I cannot change that which worries me, I forget it and let the WORRY WOCK worry for me.

(inside)
   From this day forward, I hereby give my worries to the WORRY WOCK.

   Signed, _____

Evaluation

SESSION 1 Ages 9 to 12

Name Game

Group Discussion

Something that scares me about death...

Materials

Index cards   Writing paper   Pencils

Directions

ME BOX ACTIVITY

Each student makes a Me Box on an index card.

My most important contribution to	What I have of value to share with others
My strongest characteristic	My weakest characteristic

Share with the group.

The students list ways in which people die.

Some possibilities:

old age	childbirth	abortion
surgery	war	execution
accidents	suicide	murder

Each student is asked to name the person in his life who has died, how that person died, and what he remembers about that person.

The counselor emphasizes that it is OK to have negative as well as positive memories about the deceased.

Evaluation

NOTES:

SESSION 2 Ages 9 to 12

Name Game

**Group
Discussion**

When my _____ died, I felt...

Materials

(optional)
Writing paper
Pencils

Directions

The group members will list <u>feeling words</u> which describe how each felt at the death of his loved one.

Make a list of all the feelings.

The counselor explains how persons suffering the loss of a loved one through death usually go through five stages of grief (Kubler-Ross):

   • denial • anger • bargaining • depression • acceptance

Thinking about their own experiences, encourage the students to relate to these stages of grief.

Discuss the idea that the time spent on each stage can vary.

Discuss the idea that individuals may go through one or more stages more than once, that they should not be discouraged that feelings of grief seem to re-occur after one has thought it to be worked through.

Evaluation

NOTES:

SESSION 3 Ages 9 to 12

Name Game

Group Discussion

The most difficult emotion for me to express...

Materials

The Fall of Freddie the Leaf, video, 16 minutes.

Directions

Review with the group the different stages of grief.

View *The Fall of Freddie the Leaf* or another appropriate video selected by the counselor.

Discuss how one's behavior might be affected if he were in a particular stage of grief, unable or unwilling to move on.

Evaluation

NOTES:

SESSION 4 Ages 9 to 12

Name Game

Group Discussion

When I'm upset, the expression of kindness which I most appreciate is...

Materials

Writing paper
Pencils

Directions

The students will <u>role play</u> the following situations:

1. You must tell your 7-year-old sister that the family pet has been poisoned.

2. Your two-week old baby sister dies in the hospital today. When you come home from school, you find your mother crying.

3. Your teacher's mother died unexpectedly of a heart attack. Today is her first day back at school.

4. Your best friend is very ill in the hospital. You go to visit him. He tells you that the doctor says he will probably die before Christmas.

Each student is given the task of writing a letter of condolence to one of these grieving persons.

Share the letters with the group.

Discuss the difficulty of knowing what to say in such situations.

Discuss the importance of offering support in such situations.
Explain that support may be extended by saying "I'm sorry"; by being with the grieving person; or by giving him a card, a flower, a hug.

Evaluation

NOTES:

SESSION 5 Ages 9 to 12

Name Game

Group Discussion

If I knew exactly when I was going to die, I would...

Materials

Newspapers   Drawing paper   Pencils

Directions

OBITUARIES ACTIVITY

The students look through newspapers to locate the Obituary section. Discuss the kinds of information found there and its purpose.

EPITAPHS ACTIVITY

Discuss what each group member would like others to remember about him. Each student is assigned the task of writing his own epitaph. Given drawing paper, the child draws a tombstone, writes his name, birth date, and comments about himself.

Share epitaphs with the group.

Evaluation

NOTES:

SESSION 6 Ages 9 to 12

Name Game

Group Discussion

What I've learned about death.

Materials

None.

Directions

LIFE RAFT EXPERIENCE

All the members of the group are in danger of being washed out to sea. Only three will fit on the ship's life raft, which is the only chance for survival. Each group member gets an opportunity to express his feelings about wanting to be allowed to live or to be left behind to die. The group must choose three survivors.

TENDER TOUCH ACTIVITY

Conclude this session with the Tender Touch activity. The group members stand in a line, one behind the other. The first person turns and walks to the back of the line <u>slowly</u>. As he passes the other group members, each reaches out, touches him, and says something positive about him.

Evaluation

NOTES:

SESSION 7 Ages 9 to 12

Name Game

Group Discussion

Death is...

Materials

Writing paper
Pencils
Krementz, Jill. *How It Feels When a Parent Dies*.

Directions

Conclude the sessions by reading portions of *How It Feels When a Parent Dies*.

Discuss the cycle of life and death and the inevitability of each.

LAST WILL AND TESTAMENT ACTIVITY

Each student writes a last will and testament, giving his most treasured possessions to specific persons in his life.

Share with the group.

Evaluation

NOTES:

ADDITIONAL RESOURCES

Books

Ages 6 to 8:

Center for Attitudinal Healing. *Another Look at the Rainbow*.

Center for Attitudinal Healing. *There Is a Rainbow Behind Every Dark Cloud*.

Clardy, A. *Dusty Was My Friend*.

Fassler, Joan. *The Boy With a Problem*.

Simon, Norma. *The Saddest Time*.

Viorst, Judith. *The Tenth Good Thing About Barney*.

Ages 9 to 12:

Krementz, J., *How It Feels When a Parent Dies*.

Bernstein, J., *Loss and How to Cope With It*.

Video

The Fall of Freddie the Leaf, 16 minutes.

Decision Making Group

OBJECTIVES

1. To identify the steps in decision-making.
2. To identify emotions which might influence decisions made in given social situations.
3. To make decisions within given social situations individually and as a group.
4. To identify consequences most likely to result from a decision made in a given social situation.
5. To use valuing skills which are applicable in decision-making situations.
6. To identify available resources for help in making important decisions.

Target Group

Ages 9 to 12; 6-10 students per group.

Time Requirement

45 minutes per session; 6 sessions.

Whenever you see Name Game, it means:

A simple procedure whereby the first person says, "My name is _____. What is your name?" as she turns to the person on her left. That person says, "My name is _____. Her name is _____. What is your name?" as he turns to the person on his left. And so it goes around the circle.

Whenever you see Evaluation, it means:

At the end of each group session the counselor asks individuals if they feel they have worked toward the goals of the group during that session. The counselor also asks the group members if the individual has done so. There must be a consensus that a person has cooperated and contributed to the group in order for that person to mark his success card with a smiley face.

Students who are disruptive or indifferent may not mark their cards. In the event of a disagreement over the student's eligibility for a smiley face, the counselor has the final say.

This Evaluation activity concludes each session. The counselor may extend it further by setting five smiley faces as a goal for a special reward (pencil, eraser, note pad, discount ticket for a hamburger, etc.)

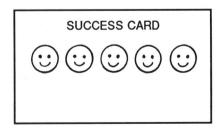

SESSION 1

Name Game

Group Discussion

Some decisions I make for myself.

Materials

None.

Directions

"ME" DECISIONS

The counselor designates opposite corners of the room as the identification areas for the choices in the following statements.

The students go to the corner which describes them best.

Are you more:

McDonald's or Pizza Hut   a rose or a dandelion
VW or Cadillac   a bat or a ball
breakfast or supper   giver or taker
pencil or pen   snowflake or dew
violet or yellow   apple or peach
snake or jackrabbit   leader or follower
Cinderella or Sleeping Beauty

Discuss the students' responses.

Administer the following test orally. Ask students to explain their answers.

GOOD OR BAD DECISIONS TEST

1. Dennis has homework to do. He is expected to have it finished by the time his mother gets home from work. His friend, Sam, calls and asks him to go to the park. He says they will be back in one hour so Dennis will have time to finish his work. Dennis decides to stay home and finish his work.

   Was this a good or bad decision? Why?

2. Sally and Lynn are in a Seven-Eleven store. While Sally is paying for her candy, she notices Lynn putting a comb in her pocketbook. As they leave the store, Sally wants to let Lynn know she has seen her but she is afraid the clerk will hear her. She decides to say nothing.

Was this a good or bad decision? Why?

3. Pets are not allowed on the beach. There is a big fine if the police catch anyone bringing a dog down to run on the sand. Bill is going to the beach to run. His dog, Biscuit, loves to run at his heels. Bill reasons that if he keeps Biscuit on a leash, it will be okay. <u>He decides to take Biscuit to the beach.</u>

Was this a good or bad decision? Why?

4. Mrs. Cook is bathing her little boy, Henry, in the bathtub. The telephone rings. Mrs. Cook hesitates before leaving Henry to answer the phone. There is just a little bit of water in the tub and she is expecting an important call from the doctor. The phone is ringing for the fourth time. Mrs. Cook looks at Henry playing nicely in the tub. <u>She decides to let the phone ring.</u>

Was this a good or bad decision? Why?

5. Alice is very interested in the boys, especially Joe. Her mother has talked to her about becoming too interested too quickly. She has forbidden her to talk to boys on the phone. Alice's mother has gone to the store and will not be home for two hours. Alice realizes she does not have her homework assignment written down. <u>She decides to call Joe to ask him the assignment.</u>

Was this a good or bad decision? Why?

6. JoAnn and Peter are cooking supper as a surprise for their parents who are still at work. Their Uncle Joshua stops by to show off his new car. He invites them to go for a ride. The children explain that they have food cooking on the stove and in the oven. Uncle Joshua tells them to turn the burner and oven down to low until they get home and everything will be fine. JoAnn and Peter's parents have talked to them a lot about the danger of fire. <u>JoAnn and Peter decide to take turns going for a ride.</u>

Was this a good or bad decision? Why?

7. Mr. Appleby gives very hard tests. This one seems to be especially difficult for Kim. She thought she had studied enough. Jackie, who sits next to Kim, is working rapidly. Kim thinks that it must be very easy for Jackie. As Jackie finishes, she asks permission to be excused, leaving her answer sheet in plain sight on her desk. Kim is tempted just this once to

borrow some answers from Jackie. Mr. Appleby has been called to the door. Everyone else is busy working. <u>Kim decides to keep working on her own.</u>

Was this a good or bad decision? Why?

8. Harry has noticed a rash on his stomach. It seems to be getting worse. He probably should see a doctor but he's afraid his parents won't let him go on a camping trip this weekend if it's something contagious. <u>Harry decides to say nothing until after this weekend.</u>

Was this a good or bad decision? Why?

9. Michelle has an Uncle Ted who is always clowning around. Everyone thinks he's funny. Lately, however, he's been hugging Michelle against him and giving her more than friendly kisses. This has made Michelle very uncomfortable. Michelle hesitates to tell her mother because Uncle Ted is her mother's brother. "After all, Uncle Ted probably doesn't mean anything by his friendliness", Michelle reasons. He says she is his favorite niece. <u>Michelle decides to talk with her school counselor about the situation.</u>

Was this a good or bad decision? Why?

10. Lacey has invited Melanie to go skating on Saturday. Both girls have been looking forward to it. Patty just found out her family has an extra ticket to the Michael Jackson concert. She calls up Melanie and invites her. Melanie doesn't know what to do. She would love to see Michael Jackson but she did make a commitment to Lacey first. <u>Melanie decides to talk with Lacey about the situation before giving Patty a final answer.</u>

Was this a good or bad decision? Why?

Evaluation

NOTES:

SESSION 2

Name Game

Group Discussion

An easy decision I have made for myself...

Materials

None.

Directions

Discuss with the group the fact that each person makes numerous decisions for himself daily.

Have each person list as many as he can remember that he has made in the course of that day.

Outline the various steps that go into making a decision:

    1. Identify the decision to be made.
    2. Identify the choices (alternatives).
    3. Consider the consequences of each alternative.
    4. Decide which would be the <u>best</u> choice.
    5. Make your decision.

Use the following example to work through the process.

    Every time Mrs. Snyder leaves the room, Christopher begins bossing everyone around. Christopher is a natural leader and most of the kids like him. His bossiness has turned into harassment. He demands that his classmates choose him, vote for him, give to him, etc. He says if anyone tells on him, he or one of his friends will beat the snitch up and he'll turn his friends against that person.

    What would you decide to do in this situation?

Encourage the students to present other situations in which decisions need to be made.

Evaluation

NOTES:

SESSION 3

Name Game

Group Discussion

A difficult decision I've made.

Materials

Writing paper

Directions

Review with the group the steps involved in making a decision. Present the two situations below. The students may choose one of these situations or one of their own. Allow each student to work through the process on paper, using the format below.

Work Sheet

DECISION-MAKING

1. What decision needs to be made?

2. What are the choices?

3. What is the consequence of each choice?

4. What would be the best choice?

5. My choice would be _____.

Share with the group.

SITUATION #1:

Shirley makes an appointment to see the school counselor. She is very nervous when she comes into the room. She begins asking the counselor to promise that she will not tell anyone that she was the one who shared this information. The counselor reassures her that information shared with her is confidential unless the safety of a student is in question, in which case the counselor might have to ask someone else to help. Shirley goes on to explain that Mr. Ruggs, her teacher, has been using profanity in the classroom and that he has been calling his students "stupid", "dumb", and "blockheads".

Shirley says the class is very upset about it and she herself is turning into a nervous wreck. She talked with her mother and her mother suggested she talk with the school counselor.

If you were the counselor, what would you do?

SITUATION #2:

Miguel has wanted to play football for a long time. This year he will be a tenth grader and finally old enough to play. The school system has a 2.0 grade point average for eligibility. Miguel just made it last spring when his grades averaged to a 2.01. His coach was thrilled because Miguel promises to be a good player. Over the summer, Miguel receives a letter from one of his teachers stating that a mistake had been made on one of his grades...that it was a D instead of a C. Miguel hurriedly computes his overall average and is sick to find it is only a 1.82. If the coach finds out, he'll know Miguel is no longer eligible to play football. Miguel is not sure the coach will know unless he tells him. Miguel has worked all summer lifting weights, getting in shape for the fall season.

If you were Miguel, what would you do?

Evaluation

NOTES:

SESSION 4

Name Game

Group Discussion

A decision I've made which affected others.

Materials

None.

Directions

GROUP DECISION-MAKING ACTIVITY

Divide the group into two smaller groups.

Explain group rules:

1. All members must agree on an answer to each question.
2. When they have reached a consensus, all group members raise their hands.
3. When the counselor sees the raised hands, she will go to the group and ask the question. She will count to three. On "three" all group members must repeat the group's decision in unison. If anyone does not answer, the counselor will assume it is not a unanimous decision and will give the group more time to work on it.

The counselor tells the students:

Task #1: "Your first task as a group is to select a leader for your group. When you have agreed upon someone, raise your hands."

When the group completes task #1, the counselor assigns that group task #2, etc.

Task #2: "You have won an all-expense paid vacation. Your second task is to decide where you would like to go."

Task #3: "Decide how you will travel there."

Task #4: "What will you do on your vacation once you arrive?"

Task #5: "You will be bringing back a souvenir from your trip. What will it be?"

Task #6: "If you could describe your trip in one word, what would it be?"

When both groups have finished or when time has expired, discuss the following questions with the entire group.

1. Did my group make decisions?
2. Was my leader fair?
3. Did I get a chance to express my opinions?
4. Did everyone in my group contribute to the decisions?
5. Do I enjoy working in a group to make decisions?
6. What are some situations when it might be advantageous to work in a group to make decisions?
7. What obstacles, if any, kept my group from performing more efficiently?
8. What happened when or if a group member refused to compromise?
9. Is decision-making more difficult within a group?

Evaluation

NOTES:

SESSION 5

Name Game

**Group
Discussion**

A decision I wish I could change...

Materials

None.

Directions

Discuss the importance of knowing oneself and one's values before making important decisions.

Explain that sometimes choices are made between two desirable alternatives; sometimes between two undesirable alternatives (this is known as choosing the lesser of two evils); and sometimes between alternatives that represent immediate gratification and delayed gratification.

Present the list below and ask each student to voice his choice. Discuss.

pizza or hamburger	a shot in the arm or in the behind
being scared or being sad	one "A" and one "C" or two "B"'s
a puppy or a kitten	being overweight or being sick
having a spoiled friend or	job now or a college education
having no friend	$5 in your hand or $5 in the bank
suspension or paddling	Six Flags or Disney World
flowers in your hand or	detention or telling on friends
flowers in your yard	no homework or good grades
$100 or one wish	Summer or Christmas

Rank in order of importance to you:

friends	new car	good reputation
family harmony	money	pet
dancing ability	good grades	good health
popularity		

Discuss your rankings.

Evaluation

NOTES:

SESSION 6

Name Game

Group Discussion

The most important decision I expect to make in my lifetime.

Materials

You Can Choose! Being Responsible, video, 25 minutes.

Directions

The group views *You Can Choose! Being Responsible* or another video on decision-making which is open-ended. Encourage discussion as to the appropriate decision to make.

Students share their life goals and some of the decisions they expect to face along the way toward realizing them.

Evaluation

NOTES:

ADDITIONAL RESOURCES

Books

Kaufman, G. & Raphael, L. *Stick Up For Yourself.*

Scott, S. *Too Smart For Trouble.*

Scott S. *How to Say No and Keep Your Friends.*

Video

Acting On Your Values, 30 minutes.

The Power of Choice, 60 minutes.

You Are Special!, 15 minutes.

You Can Choose! Being Responsible, 25 minutes.

Children of Divorce Group

OBJECTIVES

1. To discuss realistically facts about divorce.
2. To share, identify, and accept one's feelings about divorce.
3. To recognize and cope with situations and difficulties relating to divorce.
4. To develop positive personal relationships among family and friends.
5. To interact with and support other children who are experiencing divorce.

Target Group

Ages 6 to 8; 6-10 children per group.

Time Requirement

45 minutes per session; 6 sessions.

Target Group

Ages 9 to 12; 6-10 children per group.

Time Requirement

45-60 minutes per session; 8 sessions

This group is for students who have experienced or are experiencing divorce in their families.

Parental permission is recommended for participation in this group.

Whenever you see Name Game, it means:

A simple procedure whereby the first person says, "My name is _____. What is your name?" as she turns to the person on her left. That person says, "My name is _____. Her name is _____. What is your name?" as he turns to the person on his left. And so it goes around the circle.

Whenever you see Evaluation, it means:

At the end of each group session the counselor asks individuals if they feel they have worked toward the goals of the group during that session. The counselor also asks the group members if the individual has done so. There must be a consensus that a person has cooperated and contributed to the group in order for that person to mark his success card with a smiley face.

Students who are disruptive or indifferent cannot mark their cards. In the event of a disagreement over the student's eligibility for a smiley face, the counselor has the final say.

OBJECTIVES continued

This <u>Evaluation</u> activity concludes each session. The counselor may extend it further by setting five smiley faces as a goal for a special reward (pencil, eraser, note pad, discount ticket for a hamburger, etc.)

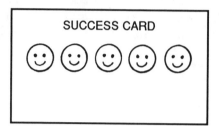

SESSION 1 Ages 6 to 8

Name Game

**Group
Discussion**

I'm _____   _____
              feeling word   child's name

Materials

5" x 7" index cards
Straight pins
Markers
Brown, L.K. & Brown, M., *Dinosaurs Divorce*

Directions

NAME TAGS

Each group member is given a 5" x 7" index card and a marker to make a name tag like the one below.

_____ Name	_____ Feeling word which describes me
_____ Favorite TV program	_____ Favorite pastime
_____ Two favorite foods	_____ Favorite color

Share name tags.

The counselor reads *Dinosaurs Divorce* or any other introductory book to divorce.

Discuss the story and relevant experiences children have had with regard to their family divorce.

Evaluation

NOTES:

SESSION 2 Ages 6 to 8

Name Game

Group Discussion

Either/Or Forced Choice Activity

Materials

Index cards from previous session
Writing paper
Crayons
Krementz, J., *How It Feels When Parents Divorce.*

Directions

On the back of the name tags from the previous session, write one word answers.

1. Whom are you closer to...   mother or father?
                                            sister or brother?

2. Which feeling describes you more often...   sad or happy?
                                            scared or brave?
                                            angry or glad?
                                            nervous or calm?

3. Would you rather be...   alone or with others?
                                            with family or with
                                                friends?
                                            at home or at school?

Share answers with the group. Participants always have the option of "passing" during sharing times.

The counselor reads some of the stories from *How It Feels When Parents Divorce.*

Discuss different feelings which are associated with divorce. The counselor makes a list of all the feeling words mentioned.

Each child chooses 5 of the feeling words to write on his FEELINGS THERMOMETER. The student colors in the thermometer to show how often he experiences each feeling.

FEELINGS THERMOMETER

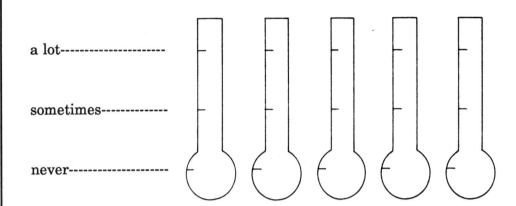

a lot----------------------

sometimes-------------

never--------------------

Evaluation

NOTES:

SESSION 3 Ages 6 to 8

Name Game

**Group
Discussion**

FAMILY PORTRAIT

Materials

Drawing paper
Crayons
A Kid's Guide to Divorce, 36 minutes, video.

Directions

Each group member draws his FAMILY PORTRAIT.

It should show the family members living in the same home with him and those who live elsewhere. The picture should be divided accordingly.

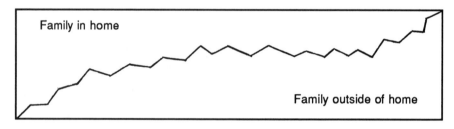

Allow each student time to share it with the group.

Discuss how the structure of the family has changed since the divorce.

View the video, *A Kid's Guide to Divorce*, or another appropriate video. Discuss any similarities between the video and each individual's situation.

Evaluation

NOTES:

SESSION 4 Ages 6 to 8

Name Game

Group Discussion

The Me Box.

Materials

| Smooth rocks | Glue | Drawing paper |
| Paint | Movable eyes | Pencils, markers |

Directions

Me Box

A good time I had with my family	An unpleasant time I had with my family
My greatest fear	My greatest hope

Share with the group.

Discuss the futility of <u>blame</u> and <u>hope for reconciliation</u>.

ANGRY STONES ACTIVITY

The group members each paint a smooth-surfaced rock, glue movable eyes on it, and paint an angry expression.

When it dries, the students practice squeezing it to allow their anger to escape down their arms and into the rocks.

Evaluation

NOTES:

SESSION 5 Ages 6 to 8

Name Game

Group Discussion

THINGS I LIKE TO DO ACTIVITY

Materials

Preprinted worksheet below
A Kid's Guide to Divorce, 36 minutes, video

Directions

Each student completes the work sheet.

Name _____
I like to do different things with different people.

Something I like to do with my sister or brother...	Something I like to do with my mother...
Something I like to do with my father...	Something I like to do with just one friend...
Something I like to do with a group of friends...	Something I like to do alone...

Share with the group.

View the relevant part of the video *A Kid's Guide to Divorce*.

Discuss the idea that the child's relationship with each parent can continue to grow, in spite of the divorce.

Evaluation

NOTES:

SESSION 6 Ages 6 to 8

Name Game

Group Discussion

Sometimes other students tease me about...

Materials

Drawing paper   Craft sticks
Crayons   Scissors
Glue

Directions

Make puppets by having children draw their own and parents' faces on paper. Cut out and glue to the craft sticks.

ROLE PLAY family situations using family-faced puppets.

1. Tell your parents the different feelings you have sometimes.

2. Tell your parents what things they do which anger you.

3. Tell your parents what you've learned about divorce.

4. Tell your parents something about yourself that they don't already know.

TENDER TOUCH ACTIVITY

The group members stand in a line, one behind the other. The first person turns and walks to the back of the line slowly. As he passes the other group members, each reaches out, touches him, and says something positive about him.

Evaluation

NOTES:

SESSION 1 Ages 9 to 12

Name Game

Group Discussion

NAME TAGS

Materials

5" x 7" index cards
Straight pins
Markers
Gardner, R. *The Boys & Girls Book About Divorce.*

Directions

NAME TAGS

Each group member is given a 5" x 7" index card and a marker to make a name tag like the one below.

_____ Name	_____ Feeling word which describes me
_____ Favorite subject	_____ Most cherished possession
_____ Best friend	_____ Goal in life

Share with the group.

Discuss the probable reasons behind divorces.

Distribute copies of Richard Gardner's *The Boys and Girls Book About Divorce* to the group members.

Homework

Read Chapters 1, 2, and 3 for the next session.

Evaluation

NOTES:

SESSION 2 Ages 9 to 12

Name Game

Group Discussion

Either/Or Forced Choice Activity

Materials

Index cards from previous session
Writing paper
Pencils
Gardner, R. *The Boys & Girls Book About Divorce.*

Directions

On the back of the name tags from the previous session, write one word answers.

1. Whom are you closer to...   mother or father?
                                        sister or brother?

2. Which feeling describes you more often...   happy or sad?
                                        angry or glad?
                                        scared or brave?
                                        nervous or calm?

3. Would you rather be...   alone or with others?
                                        with family or with
                                            friends?
                                        at home or at school?

Share answers with group. Participants always have the option of "passing" during sharing times.

The group discusses Chapters 1, 2, and 3 of Gardner's book. Emphasize the futility of hoping things will get patched up between the parents; blame; and feelings associated with divorce.

Each student makes a list of <u>feeling words</u> which he has experienced with regard to divorce. Using five of the more common ones, each student completes a FEELINGS THERMOMETER. (Refer to SESSION #2 Ages 6 to 8 on page 88.)

Homework

Read Chapter 4 in *The Boys and Girls Book About Divorce.*

Evaluation

SESSION 3 Ages 9 to 12

Name Game

Group Discussion

Something about divorce that makes me angry.

Materials

Squares of material   Needles
Pillow stuffing   Thread
Straight pins   Fabric Crayons
Thread   Iron
Gardner, R., _The Boys & Girls Book About Divorce._

Directions

Discuss reasons for feeling angry and some ways people express their anger. Emphasize the OK-ness of feeling angry.

Discuss Chapter 4 in _The Boys and Girls Book About Divorce_.

List some appropriate methods of dealing with anger.

ANGRY PILLOWS ACTIVITY

The students sew squares of material together to make a pillow or the counselor comes prepared with three sides already machine-stitched. The students, on a piece of white paper not larger than the face of the pillow, draw with fabric crayons an angry face of something about divorce which makes them angry.

The counselor helps them iron this picture on to the face of the pillow. Stuff the pillow and sew the open side closed.

Discuss the hazards of taking anger out on animate objects. Explain that taking it out on an inanimate object such as a pillow might help one to avoid hurting someone in anger.

Discuss "talking it out" as the most desirable behavior in handling angry feelings.

Put the pillows on display if the students desire. They are theirs to take home afterwards.

Homework

Read Chapter 5 in Gardner's book.

Evaluation

SESSION 4 Ages 9 to 12

Name Game

Group Discussion

FAMILY PORTRAIT and Me Box

Materials

Index cards
Pencils
Gardner, R., *The Boys & Girls Book About Divorce*.

Directions

FAMILY PORTRAIT

On one side of an index card, the students will draw or write the names of their family members, those living in the same household separated from those who live outside the household.

ME BOX

On the reverse side of the index card, members write their answers to the phrases below.

A good time I had with my family	An unpleasant time I had with my family
My greatest fear	My greatest accomplishment

Share with the group.

Discuss Chapter 5 of Gardner's book.

Homework

None.

Evaluation

NOTES:

SESSION 5 Ages 9 to 12

Name Game

Group Discussion

THINGS I LIKE TO DO ACTIVITY

Materials

Preprinted worksheet below
Gardner, R. *The Boys & Girls Book About Divorce.*

Directions

Each student completes the worksheet.

Name _____	
I like to do different things with different people.	
Something I like to do with my sister or brother...	Something I like to do with my mother...
Something I like to do with my father...	Something I like to do with just one friend...
Something I like to do with a group of friends...	Something I like to do alone...

Share with the group.

Homework

Read Chapters 6, 7, and 8 in Gardner's book.

Evaluation

NOTES:

SESSION 6 Ages 9 to 12

Name Game

Group Discussion

It's embarrassing/not embarrassing for me to have divorced parents.

Materials

Drawing paper   Glue
Pencils, crayons   Craft sticks
Gardner, R. *The Boys & Girls Book About Divorce.*

Directions

Make puppets by having children draw their own and parents' faces on paper. Cut out and glue to craft sticks.

ROLEPLAY family situations using family-faced puppets.

1. Tell your parents what you have learned about divorce.

2. Tell your parents how you <u>feel</u> about the divorce.

3. Tell your parents what they do that angers you.

4. Tell your step-parent something about yourself which he/she may not know.

Discuss Chapters 6, 7, and 8 in *The Boys and Girls Book About Divorce*.

Homework

Read Chapters 10 and 11 in Gardner's book.

Evaluation

NOTES:

SESSION 7 Ages 9 to 12

Name Game

Group Discussion

When I grow up.

Materials

None.

Directions

With the group's permission, invite a divorced adult to visit the group to share some of the adult's perspective and to answer questions from the students about divorce. It might be possible to have a school staff member be the guest if there is someone who might have already established rapport with the students and who would be willing to "risk" such sharing.

Conclude with the TENDER TOUCH ACTIVITY.

The group members stand in a line, one behind the other. The first person turns and walks to the back of the line slowly. As he passes the other group members, each reaches out, touches him, and says something positive about him. Be sure to include the visitor.

Homework

None.

Evaluation

NOTES:

SESSION 8 Ages 9 to 12

Name Game

Group Discussion

From participation in this group, I have learned...

Materials

Small, smooth rock for each student	Paint
Half sheet of 9 x 12 construction paper	Paintbrushes
Fine-line markers	Glue
Two movable eyes	

Directions

Paint the rocks. When dry, glue two eyes on each. Fold the paper for booklet. Write message written below, whisper worry to the WORRY WOCK, and sign it.

(cover)
    If I can change that which worries me, I change it.

    If I cannot change that which worries me, I forget it and let the WORRY WOCK worry for me.

(inside)
    From this day forward, I hereby give my worries to the WORRY WOCK.

    Signed, _____

Discuss relaxation and how important physical exercise is to keeping an emotional perspective on one's life.

WORRY WOCK reprinted by permission of Bammie Cofield and Ann Spencer, Counselors, Ft. Benning Dependents School.

SESSION 8 Ages 9 to 12 continued

The group will practice some relaxation exercises together: tensing and relaxing various parts of the body from the feet to the head; inhaling/exhaling; guided imageries such as walk on the beach, flying a kite, floating in an ocean, standing on top of a mountain.

Finally, the group will discuss the difference between worries they can do something about and those they can't. Each student makes a WORRY WOCK and booklet.

Homework

None.

Evaluation

NOTES:

ADDITIONAL RESOURCES

Books

Brown, L.K. & Brown, M., *Dinosaurs Divorce.*

Gardner, R. *The Boys & Girls Book About Divorce.*

Holland, R. *About Me.*

Ives, S., Fassler, D., & Lach, M. *Changing Families.*

Ives, S., Fassler, D., & Lach, M. *The Divorce Workbook.*

Johnson, Linda. *Your Parents Divorce.*

Krementz, Jill. *How It Feels When Parents Divorce.*

Rofes, Eric, Editor. *The Kids Book of Divorce.*

Sanford, Doris. *Please Come Home.*

Simon, Norma. *All Kinds of Families.*

Simon, Norma. *I Wish I Had My Father.*

Video

A Kid's Guide to Divorce, 36 minutes.

No Fault Kids, 30 minutes.

Jogging Group

OBJECTIVES

1. To provide "time out" from the traditional closed-space school environment.
2. To teach children running as a sport and a leisure time activity.
3. To provide a release for anxiety and anger through physical activity.
4. To teach proper techniques of exercising and running.
5. To improve self-concept through personal accomplishment.

Target Group

Ages 9 to 12; 10-15 students per group.

Time Requirement

60 minutes per session; 6 sessions.

Other Requirements

Parental permission, a family doctor's clearance, and appropriate shoes.

Whenever you see Name Game, it means:

A simple procedure whereby the first person says, "My name is _____. What is your name?" as she turns to the person on her left. That person says, "My name is _____. Her name is _____. What is your name?" as he turns to the person on his left. And so it goes around the circle.

Whenever you see Evaluation, it means:

At the end of each group session the counselor asks individuals if they feel they have worked toward the goals of the group during that session. The counselor also asks the group members if the individual has done so. There must be a consensus that a person has cooperated and contributed to the group in order for that person to mark his success card with a smiley face.

Students who are disruptive or indifferent may not mark their cards. In the event of a disagreement over the student's eligibility for a smiley face, the counselor has the final say.

This Evaluation activity concludes each session. The counselor may extend it further by setting five smiley faces as a goal for a special reward (pencil, eraser, note pad, discount ticket for a hamburger, etc.)

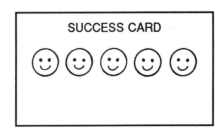

107

SESSION 1

Name Game

**Group
Discussion**

An overview of running.

Materials

None.

Directions

A representative from a local running organization is invited to visit the group to introduce the sport of running. He presents some personal history of his interest in running.

The students explain their reasons for wanting to learn more about running. Some of those reasons might include an interest in the sport, a desire to expend some energy in an appropriate way, and a desire to experience success in some aspect of school.

The resource speaker shows a film which gives a general overview of running. He explains some of the reasons other people have become interested in running.

The speaker discusses appropriate clothing and shoes for running in different types of weather. The emphasis is on minimal expense.

The speaker entertains questions from the group.

Homework

None.

Evaluation

NOTES:

SESSION 2

Name Game

Group Discussion

Getting started...warm-up exercises.

Materials

Log book for each member.

Directions

The P.E. teacher teaches the student how to take their pulse. The students record it in their log book.

Date	Pulse (Before exercise)	Distance	Pulse (After exercise)

The P.E. teacher discusses the importance of warming up with stretching exercises before running and cooling down after running.

The P.E. teacher teaches the students some warm-up exercises.

SIT-UPS to strengthen stomach muscles and stretch hamstring and calf muscles. Lie on your back with your right knee flexed, foot on the floor, and your left leg straight. Slowly raise your left leg until it is perpendicular to the floor and your toes are pointing straight up. Lower your left leg slowly and repeat the whole sequence with your right leg. Stretch both legs 3 or 4 times.

FACE A WALL, put your palms against it, slowly shuffle backward, keeping your feet flat on the ground, until you feel strain in the back of your legs. Hold this position.

LIE ON YOUR back. Keep your legs together. Slowly bring them over your head and with your knees straight, hold your feet parallel to the floor for 20 seconds.

109

SESSION 2 continued

PUT PALMS against a wall. Slide one foot back and keep leg straight, foot flat on floor. Bend front leg and lunge forward toward the wall. Alternate legs.

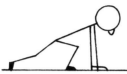

SQUAT STRETCH with hands parallel on floor, shoulder width apart. Keep right leg bent forward under body, foot flat on the floor. Left leg should be extended with toes flat on the floor. Stretch. Alternate legs and repeat.

The students take their pulse again after doing exercises and record the data in their log books.

Homework

Students are to do these warm-up exercises at least three times during the coming week.

Evaluation

NOTES:

SESSION 3

Name Game

**Group
Discussion**

Time for running...

Materials

Log books

Directions

The counselor introduces the concept of running styles to the students. Some important points might be:

1. <u>Individual</u> styles will develop.
2. A runner should touch down on the flat of the foot, roll his weight forward from heel to toe.
3. Knees should be flexed.
4. Lean forward slightly so that weight is over the front foot.
5. Arms will be bent at 90° angle, close to the body.
6. Hands, jaw, and shoulders are relaxed.

Students take and record pulse.

Students do the warm-up exercises.

The group goes out to the school yard and assembles.

Students with the counselor and P.E. teacher will walk, run, walk, etc., once around the half mile yard.

The group will then walk around the yard once to cool down.

Runners take their pulse again and record it.

Runners should also record in their log the nature of their run, the distance, and any comment about their perception of it.

Date	Distance	Location	Method	Comments
9/7/84	1/2 mile	Penn Ave Sch.	Run, walk	Enjoyed it. Felt tired at the end.

Students should share their reactions to their first run.

Homework

None.

SESSION 3 continued

Evaluation

NOTES:

SESSION 4

Name Game

Group Discussion

Potential problems...

Materials

Log books

Directions

A medical doctor who also runs is invited to speak to the group about ways to prevent injuries, what the common injuries are, and how to recuperate from injuries.

His talk should include:

blisters	side stitch	cramps and spasms
black toe	jogger's heel	achilles tendonitis
shin splints	dehydration	knee injuries

Group members take their pulse and record it.

The students do their warm-up exercises.

The students run, walk, run, walk, etc. once around the school yard.

The students walk around the yard once for their cool-down walk.

The students take their pulse and record it.

The students record their run in their logs.

Homework

The students are to run, walk, the same distance on alternate days (three days) before the next group meeting, as well as continue to do the warm-up exercises.

Evaluation

NOTES:

SESSION 5

Name Game

Group Discussion

Jogging and your weight.

Materials

Log books

Directions

A representative from the local running club speaks with the group about body builds and weight (according to doctor's charts). Running is discussed in terms of conditioning and calorie consumption. Appropriate ways to maintain, lose or gain weight are discussed.

Students are weighed and measured. They record their measurements in their log books.

DATE	HEIGHT	WEIGHT

Students compare their measurements to the charts. No weight reduction will be recommended, but if a student expresses an interest, he will be referred to his family doctor.

Students record their pulse.

Warm-up exercises.

Run, walk, run, walk around the school grounds twice.

Cool-down, walk once around the yard.

Students record pulse.

Students record run in their log books.

Homework

Students should run three times during the week and record each in their log books.

Evaluation

SESSION 6

Name Game

Group Discussion

Keeping it up.

Materials

Log books

Directions

The group members discuss how they feel about running.

Students take their pulse and record it.

Warm-up exercises.

The students run twice around the yard.

Cool-down walk once around the yard.

Students take pulse and record it.

Students record run in their log books.

Ribbons are awarded to students who have attended each of the group sessions and participated in each run.

Plans are made to continue the weekly runs at a regular meeting time. Distance is gradually increased.

A goal will be to take those students who stay with the running to a community fun run.

Homework

Continue with the program.

Evaluation

NOTES:

ADDITIONAL RESOURCES

Video

Coping With Pressures, 30 minutes.

Relax - Slim Goodbody, 15 minutes.

Take It Easy, 19 minutes.

Teenage Stress, 28 minutes.

Motivation Group

OBJECTIVES

1. To identify specific areas of school behavior which need improvement.
2. To assist children in being accountable for their academic and social behaviors.
3. To provide positive reinforcement for behavior which approximates appropriate school expectations.
4. To assist children to develop self-discipline for accomplishing assigned academic or behavioral tasks.

Target Group

Ages 6 to 12

Time Requirement

15-30 minute sessions; daily sessions initially, tapering off to weekly or bi-weekly sessions as the child improves.

Whenever you see Name Game, it means:

A simple procedure whereby the first person says, "My name is _____. What is your name?" as she turns to the person on her left. That person says, "My name is _____ _____. Her name is _____. What is your name?" as he turns to the person on his left. And so it goes around the circle.

Whenever you see Evaluation, it means:

At the end of each group session the counselor asks individuals if they feel they have worked toward the goals of the group during that session. The counselor also asks the group members if the individual has done so. There must be a consensus that a person has cooperated and contributed to the group in order for that person to mark his success card with a smiley face.

Students who are disruptive or indifferent may not mark their cards. In the event of a disagreement over the student's eligibility for a smiley face, the counselor has the final say.

This Evaluation activity concludes each session. The counselor may extend it further by setting five smiley faces as a goal for a special reward (pencil, eraser, note pad, discount ticket for a hamburger, etc.)

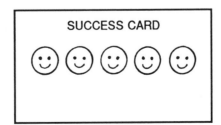

SESSION 1 (and follow-up sessions)

Name Game

**Group
Discussion**

None.

Materials

Success Card

Directions

Once the student has been referred to the counselor, the teacher, the student and the counselor attempt to identify specific areas which need to be monitored. These specific behaviors are recorded on a success card.

SUCCESS CARD					
Homework turned in					
Begins work immediately					
Listens to directions					
Completes work					
Shows good effort					

SUCCESS CARD					
Stays in seat					
Stays in classroom					
Raises hand to speak					
Responds cheerfully					
Takes care of property					

The teacher, the student, or both may have the responsibility of marking the card each day. The student brings the card to the counselor at the end of the day. The group members report on their activities and progress for the day.

Three out of five areas checked as satisfactory, the student may be allowed to put a star on the Star Student Chart in the counselor's office. If the individual has not met his goal, he discusses what obstacles stood in his way. The students then set their goals for the next day.

Initially, goals may include obtaining one check out of five. As the student continues in the group, his expectations will be greater. Once he consistently meets an objective, that objective may be dropped and another substituted for it.

At the end of each week (or a designated time period) the counselor may send a Happy Gram note home to the student's parents to tell them about the child's progress.

As the group members improve, the meeting time may be reduced to three times a week, then once a week, then once every two weeks, etc. until the need to meet ceases to exist.

As opportunities arise for children to assume special responsibilities within the school such as Master of Ceremonies at assemblies, office helper, greeter for school guests, etc. these students who have demonstrated some growth in personal motivation may be considered for such honors.

The end-of-the-year awards assembly might be another appropriate time to recognize these "motivation masters" in some positive way.

Evaluation

NOTES:

ADDITIONAL RESOURCES

Books

Canfield, J., _100 Ways to Enhance Self-Esteem in the Classroom._

Haag, K., et. al., _Common Solutions for the Uncommon Child._

Video

You Can Choose! Being Responsible, 25 minutes.

Peer
Relations
Group

OBJECTIVES

1. To learn how others perceive one's self.
2. To practice appropriate ways of relating to others.
3. To explore alternate ways of dealing with unsatisfactory peer relationships.
4. To experience how it feels to be left out.
5. To discuss prejudice and how it affects others.

Target Group

Ages 6 to 12; 6-10 students per group.

Time Requirement

30-45 minutes per session; 7 sessions.

Whenever you see <u>Name Game</u>, it means:

A simple procedure whereby the first person says, "My name is _____. What is your name?" as she turns to the person on her left. That person says, "My name is _____. Her name is _____. What is your name?" as he turns to the person on his left. And so it goes around the circle.

Whenever you see <u>Evaluation</u>, it means:

At the end of each group session the counselor asks individuals if they feel they have worked toward the goals of the group during that session. The counselor also asks the group members if the individual has done so. There must be a consensus that a person has cooperated and contributed to the group in order for that person to mark his success card with a smiley face.

Students who are disruptive or indifferent may not mark their cards. In the event of a disagreement over the student's eligibility for a smiley face, the counselor has the final say.

This <u>Evaluation</u> activity concludes each session. The counselor may extend it further by setting five smiley faces as a goal for a special reward (pencil, eraser, note pad, discount ticket for a hamburger, etc.)

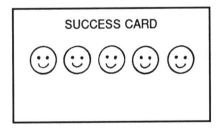

SESSION 1

Name Game

Group Discussion

A situation in which I find it difficult to get along with others.

Materials

Acting on Your Values, 30 minutes, video.
Dealing With Feelings, 25 minutes, video.

Directions

Lemonland Activity

The counselor reads the story <u>Lemonland</u>, below.

LEMONLAND

Funny or not?

Imagine for a moment. You are from Lemonland. You are called a Lemonite. Other people from your land are called Lemonites too. One day a friend who is not from Lemonland tells a joke.

What did the bully say about the people in Lemonland?

You say, "I don't know."

And he says, "They're yellow through and through."

Your friend is roaring with laughter. Are you? Do you think this joke is funny? Would the other people who live in Lemonland think it was funny? Did it hurt your feelings?

People often tell jokes about groups - religious, national, racial, sexist. These jokes are often based on some feature or difference that the group has. Sometimes the same joke might be used for a few groups by just changing names. Do <u>you</u> tell jokes like this?

Do you think jokes like this help people understand each other better through laughter? Why or why not? Would it be different if someone from your own group told a joke about the group? Why?

The students view either *Dealing With Feelings*, or *Acting on Your Values*, or another relevant video which dramatizes typical school problems which require decision-making.

Discuss.

SESSION 1 continued

<u>Evaluation</u>

<u>NOTES:</u>

SESSION 2

Name Game

**Group
Discussion**

When I choose a new friend, I look for someone who...

Materials

Helena, Ann, *The Lie*

Directions

BIBLIOTHERAPY

The counselor reads a story, *The Lie*, to the group. *The Lie* is a story about a girl who puts on her friend's necklace to admire it, but without permission. When she is taking it off, it slips and breaks. Her friend discovers it and the teacher has asked the guilty party to own up to the act.

Discuss what made the character lie (fear of having her best friend angry with her or dislike her). Since the story is open-ended, the students can suggest how they might have handled the situation.

ROLE PLAY

Role play various solutions to this situation.

The counselor presents any/all of the problem situations listed below.

The students role play the situations and then discuss reasons for inappropriate behavior and appropriate alternatives.

Situations:

1. George makes a nuisance of himself. He interrupts conversation and always has to be first in line.
2. Martha sings and taps at her desk while others are working. She says it helps her to think more clearly.
3. Lee is always in a hurry. He runs down the halls and walkways, nearly knocking people over. He cuts in line at lunch, at the water fountain, and at the bathroom.
4. Jean daydreams a lot. She never quite gets started on her work until a few people have already finished. Then she asks them to help her. She says she doesn't understand or remember the directions.

Evaluation

SESSION 3

Name Game

Group Discussion

A time when I wanted to be leader.

Materials

Five headbands with phrases as indicated

Directions

BRAINSTORMING PROBLEM SITUATIONS

Problem: More than one person in the group wants to be the leader. Brainstorm ways to choose a leader. Role play each suggestion. For example:

    Pulling name out of a hat
    "Eenie meenie miney mo" rhymes
    Person in center of a circle closes his eyes and spins around and
        points to one member of the group
    Make a list of names and go in order
    Pull straws
    Guess a number from 1 to 10
    "Awka bawka soda cracker"
    ABC order

HEADBAND ACTIVITY

One student volunteers to leave the room. The counselor shows the group one of the following headbands:

    IGNORE ME
    GIVE ME WARM FUZZIES
    DISAGREE WITH EVERYTHING I SAY
    SMILE AT ME WHEN I TALK
    AGREE WITH EVERYTHING I SAY

The counselor explains that while the group is discussing a topic, the group members should respond to the individual wearing the headband by doing what the headband says.

Invite the student in. Put the headband on him without his seeing it. Begin a discussion about school, parents, report cards, vacation, etc. After a given period of time, stop the discussion and ask the headband wearer how he perceived what was happening. Elicit his feelings about having been ignored, disagreed with, etc.

Repeat the activity with another student and another headband.

When all the headbands have been used, discuss how we can affect others' behavior by how we relate to them.

Evaluation

NOTES:

SESSION 4

Name Game

Group Discussion

A time when I felt left out or when I caused someone else to feel left out...

Materials

Many small pieces of blue and green tape
One piece of yellow tape
"Fact or Prejudice" worksheets

Directions

PREJUDICE ACTIVITY

Ask the group to close its eyes. Explain that the counselor will come by and put a piece of tape on each person's forehead. One person will receive the yellow tape but the group will not know this. With eyes remained closed, each student should decide whether he feels more "blue" or "green". If he feels "blue" he should move to a particular side of the room which has been designated the "blue" side. If he feels "green" he should move to the "green" side of the room. WITHOUT ANY VERBAL COMMUNICATION the students should help each other get to the proper side of the room.

What will happen is that the person with the yellow square of tape will be pushed from group to group, figuratively speaking. He will not fit in. He does not know his color is different.

Follow the activity with a discussion of how it feels to be the different person. Ask the rest of the group to express their feelings on what they saw happening. Discuss being different, leaving someone out, and the meaning of prejudice.

For students 9 to 12 years old, conclude with the Fact or Prejudice Worksheet on the next page, to further reinforce these two concepts.

Discuss the students' answers.

Evaluation

NOTES:

WORKSHEET

FACT OR PREJUDICE?

(Put an F or P before each statement)

_____   1.   Mrs. Wright is a great teacher!

_____   2.   I'm going to do poorly in this class. I always do!

_____   3.   Mary Ann started that rumor. She always does!

_____   4.   I love chocolate ice cream!

_____   5.   My baby sister weights 13 pounds and has red hair.

_____   6.   Mr. Gregg always picks Gary for special jobs because he's the teacher's pet.

_____   7.   He thinks he's so cool.

_____   8.   My mother says you can't trust anybody who lives in that neighborhood.

_____   9.   Jeff is the tallest boy in our class.

_____ 10.   I don't like her because she has buck teeth.

_____ 11.   If you study hard, you may get good grades.

_____ 12.   Don't pick him for our team; he can't hit the ball.

_____ 13.   Susie is such a loudmouth; she can't keep a secret.

_____ 14.   Mrs. Davenport has three children.

_____ 15.   White people are prejudiced against blacks.

_____ 16.   Short basketball players usually cheat.

_____ 17.   Jewish people are tight with their money.

_____ 18.   We live in a city near the ocean.

_____ 19.   Don't go to her house; it's filled with lice.

_____ 20.   He wears glasses; he must be a sissy.

SESSION 5

Name Game

Group Discussion

A time when it was difficult for me to wait my turn.

Materials

Video about taking turns and playing fair
UNGAME

Directions

View video about taking turns and playing fair.

Discuss.

Play the UNGAME or any other game in which there is no clearly defined winner.

Discuss why this game is different from other games.

Discuss why being the winner is not always important.

Emphasize the importance of following rules, taking turns, etc.

Evaluation

NOTES:

SESSION 6

Name Game

Group Discussion

A time when I controlled/did not control my emotions.

Materials

Self-hardening clay
Pencils

Directions

CONCENTRATION ACTIVITY

The children hurl insults, tease, etc. at a student volunteer. The volunteer concentrates and tries to keep a straight face. He blocks out their insults and refuses to react in any way. Afterwards, the group members discuss what it feels like to be teased and to be ignored. The students discuss different situations where ignoring the perpetrator might be advantageous.

Given a glob of clay, each student shapes it into a face. He uses a pencil to draw the features. After it dries, the student takes it home as a reminder that ignoring others' inappropriate behaviors is sometimes the most effective way of discouraging them.

Evaluation

NOTES:

SESSION 7

Name Game

Group Discussion

Cooperation is...

Materials

Two envelopes each containing five cut-up squares

Directions

COOPERATIVE SQUARES ACTIVITY

Divide the group into 2 smaller groups. Each group receives an envelope with 5 paper squares which have been cut into several pieces inside. The directions say that the group members are to assemble their squares as quickly as possible without any verbal communication.

Following the activity, discussion should include:

1. Did our group reach its goal of assembling the squares without verbal communication?

2. Did we have to share with each other?

3. What were the results of the sharing or lack of it?

4. Did any members of our group refuse to cooperate? With what results?

5. When is it important for people to cooperate?

6. When is it almost impossible to get a task done without cooperation?

Repeat the cooperative squares activity and discuss any differences the second time through.

Evaluation

NOTES:

Squares Patterns to be used for Cooperative Squares:

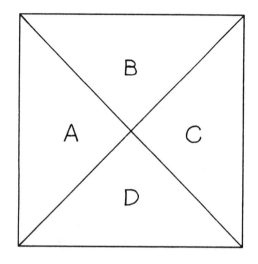

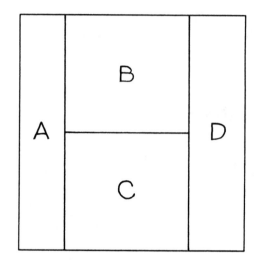

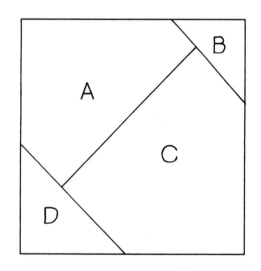

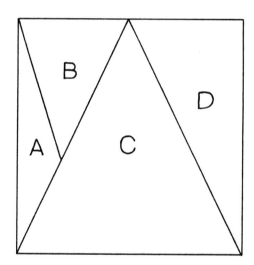

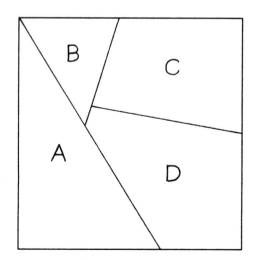

ADDITIONAL RESOURCES

<u>Books</u>

Crary, Elizabeth. *My Name Is Not Dummy*.

Helena, Ann. *The Lie*.

Holland, R. *About Me.*

<u>Games</u>

UNGAME

<u>Video</u>

Acting On Your Values, 30 minutes.

Dealing With Feelings, 25 minutes.

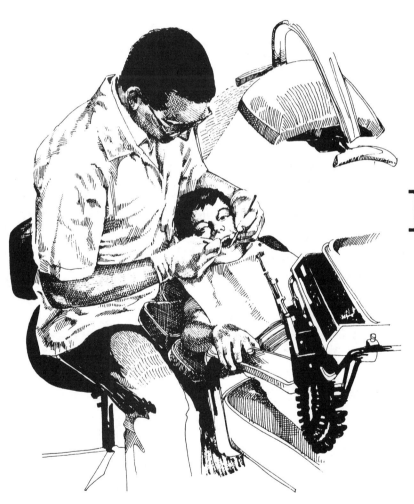

Personal Hygiene Group

OBJECTIVES

1. To become aware of specific personal hygiene needs.
2. To perform hands-on hygiene activities.
3. To discuss the consequences of poor hygiene.
4. To develop pride in one's appearance.
5. To strengthen one's self-concept.

Target Group

Ages 6 to 12; 6-10 students per group.

This group is targeted for students who have had little support in the area of personal hygiene and who need instruction in very basic areas.

Time Requirement

45 minutes per session; 7 sessions.

Whenever you see Name Game, it means:

A simple procedure whereby the first person says, "My name is _____. What is your name?" as she turns to the person on her left. That person says, "My name is _____. Her name is _____. What is your name?" as he turns to the person on his left. And so it goes around the circle.

Whenever you see Evaluation, it means:

At the end of each group session the counselor asks individuals if they feel they have worked toward the goals of the group during that session. The counselor also asks the group members if the individual has done so. There must be a consensus that a person has cooperated and contributed to the group in order for that person to mark his success card with a smiley face.

Students who are disruptive or indifferent may not mark their cards. In the event of a disagreement over the student's eligibility for a smiley face, the counselor has the final say.

This Evaluation activity concludes each session. The counselor may extend it further by setting five smiley faces as a goal for a special reward (pencil, eraser, note pad, discount ticket for a hamburger, etc.)

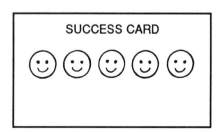

141

SESSION 1

Name Game

Group Discussion

I am important because...

Materials

Full-length mirror
Empty deodorant, soap, mouthwash, etc. containers

Directions

The students stand one at a time in front of a full-length mirror. Each describes what he sees, what he likes best and least about his physical appearance.

The group members <u>brainstorm</u> common poor hygiene problems. Some examples might be:

bad breath	smelly clothes
oily hair	bitten, dirty nails
facial blemishes	dirty hands
body odor	

ROLE PLAY

The students pretend to be on TV performing in commercials which present answers to the problems of poor hygiene; for example, soap, mouthwash, deodorant. Empty containers for the various products might be used during the role play.

Following the activity, the counselor needs to emphasize that remediation of poor hygiene lies in practicing basic skills which the group will have a chance to practice, and not in buying costly products.

Homework

None.

Evaluation

NOTES:

SESSION 2

Name Game

Group Discussion

I like myself when...

Materials

Wash basin	Nail brushes
Warm water	Emery boards
Soap	Paper towels

Directions

HAND WASHING ACTIVITY

The counselor demonstrates how to wash one's hands thoroughly using lots of suds. The children wash their hands, rinse, and then wash again.

Using a nail brush, each child will scrub his nails, one at a time, trying hard to remove all the dirt under and around his nails. The children will wash their hands again and dry them thoroughly.

Using an emery board, the children will file their nails so as to smooth any rough or uneven spots.

Following this activity, the children will tell when and why it is important to keep one's hands clean.

Discuss washing hands before and after eating, using the bathroom, etc.

Discuss nail biting as a habit to be avoided.

Discuss the idea that our hands sometimes give others an impression as to the type of total person we are.

Homework

None.

Evaluation

NOTES:

SESSION 3

Name Game

Group Discussion

I feel encouraged when...

Materials

Wash basin	Warm water
Soap	Paper towels
Q-tips	Hand cream or moisturizing lotion

Directions

FACE AND SKIN CARE

The students will wash thoroughly with sudsy, warm water their hands, arms, and faces. Wash with circular motions on the face - wash up and out. Pat the skin dry with paper towels.

The students will massage their hands, elbows, and faces with moisturizing cream. Discuss the importance of keeping moisture in the skin - and the harmful effects sun, water, and wind can have on it.

EAR CARE

The counselor will demonstrate how to use a Q-tip and warm water to clean the <u>outer</u> ear. Emphasize the dangers of putting anything in one's ears. Discuss the importance of keeping one's ears clean as a precaution for maintaining good hearing. The students will clean their outer ears with Q-tip and warm water.

Homework

Each student is to bring one item of dirty clothing (not white) to next week's session. Each student also receives a permission slip to have signed by his parent, giving him permission to go to a local laundromat next week.

Evaluation

NOTES:

SESSION 4

Name Game

Group Discussion

Secretly, I wish...

Materials

Deodorant	Soap flakes
Dusting Powder	Antiperspirant
Perfume	Bleach
Wash basin	Coins
Warm water	Measuring Cup

Directions

BODY CLEANLINESS

The group will discuss the importance of bathing <u>daily</u> (aesthetic reasons, comfort, social value, disease prevention, etc.). For the older students, the counselor will discuss the importance of using deodorant or antiperspirant and the difference between the two. No substitutes such as dusting powder or perfume are effective to control body odor.

CLEAN CLOTHING

The group discusses the importance of wearing clean clothing <u>daily</u>. For children who sleep with younger brothers or sisters who might wet the bed, it is imperative that they wash and wear clean underwear every morning.

For students who have few pieces of clothing or whose parents are unable to wash clothes frequently, it is important that they learn to wash small items of clothing by hand and to learn to operate washing machines at a laundromat.

The counselor demonstrates how to wash a pair of socks in a basin with warm water. Rinsing the soap out is emphasized. The students practice washing socks out in the basin.

The group then goes to the neighborhood laundromat. The children practice measuring the detergent, etc. and operating the washer and dryer. The dirty items the children brought from home are washed. They carry the clean items home at the end of the day.

SESSION 4 continued

Homework

None.

Evaluation

NOTES:

SESSION 5

Name Game

Group Discussion

I'm glad when I have learned how to...

Materials

Toothbrushes   Toothpaste
Dental floss   Paper cups
Dental care booklets

Directions

DENTAL CARE

A dental hygienist student visits the group session to talk about dental hygiene. She explains the importance of caring for one's teeth and gums. She explains the physiological cause of bad breath.

The hygienist demonstrates the proper way to brush and floss teeth.

The students receive toothbrushes and toothpaste. Following the hygienist's directions, the children brush their teeth thoroughly and floss their teeth too.

The hygienist also provides the students with booklets about dental care which are theirs to share with their families.

Homework

None.

Evaluation

NOTES:

SESSION 6

Name Game

Group Discussion

Someone I admire is _____ because...

Materials

None.

Directions

HAIR CARE

A hair stylist from the community is invited to visit and talk with the students about the importance of clean hair. She explains the differences among oily, dry, and normal hair and how one can tell these differences. She shows the students different hair products and explains which basics are needed for hair care. She discusses the importance of hair care to one's appearance and feeling of general well-being and the importance of diet and the influence on one's hair.

Homework

None.

Evaluation

NOTES:

SESSION 7

Name Game

Group Discussion

If I could change one thing about myself, it would be...

Materials

None.

Directions

The last session is a wrap-up of several different hygiene practices.

The school nurse visits the group and discusses common health problems such as colds, head lice, sores, etc. She emphasizes the need to avoid sharing food or drink or combs or hats. She cautions the students about picking sores, etc.

The nurse discusses poor social hygiene habits of: chewing on things (hair, nails, pencils); picking one's nose; etc.

The group members offer their reactions to peers who conduct themselves in such inappropriate ways.

The nurse encourages questions from the students.

The group concludes with "I learned..." statements.

Homework

None.

Evaluation

NOTES:

Responsibility Group

OBJECTIVES

1. To identify self, school, and home responsibilities.
2. To be provided with responsibilities which require planning and follow-through.
3. To chart one's own progress with assuming responsibilities.
4. To identify feelings associated with responsibilities and expectations.
5. To provide positive reinforcement for successful attempts at assuming responsibility.

Target Group

Ages 6 to 12; 6-10 students per group.

Time Requirement

30-45 minutes per session; 6 sessions.

Whenever you see Name Game, it means:

A simple procedure whereby the first person says, "My name is _____. What is your name?" as she turns to the person on her left. That person says, "My name is _____. Her name is _____. What is your name?" as he turns to the person on his left. And so it goes around the circle.

Whenever you see Evaluation, it means:

At the end of each group session the counselor asks individuals if they feel they have worked toward the goals of the group during that session. The counselor also asks the group members if the individual has done so. There must be a consensus that a person has cooperated and contributed to the group in order for that person to mark his success card with a smiley face.

Students who are disruptive or indifferent may not mark their cards. In the event of a disagreement over the student's eligibility for a smiley face, the counselor has the final say.

This Evaluation activity concludes each session. The counselor may extend it further by setting five smiley faces as a goal for a special reward (pencil, eraser, note pad, discount ticket for a hamburger, etc.)

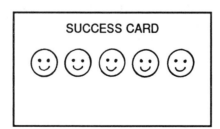

SESSION 1

Name Game

Group Discussion

Responsibility is...

Materials

Contracts
Scavenger lists

Directions

Discuss the meaning of responsibility.

Emphasize planning, commitment, and follow-through as necessary ingredients.

CONTRACTS - SCAVENGER HUNT ACTIVITY

Present a contract to each student. It is a contract for participation in a scavenger hunt. If the student agrees to sign it, he is accepting the responsibility of participating with his best effort. (All children will sign.)

(Sample)

I,_____, agree to participate in the _____ school scavenger hunt. I agree to try my best to find the items listed below in the 10 minutes allotted.   _____   _____   Date   Student's Signature

At the counselor's signal, the students and the counselor go out of the school grounds to begin the hunt. There is a 10-minute time limit. Each child receives the list and a bag with which to collect his treasures.

```
SCAVENGER LIST

Check off each item as you find it.

        handful of grass
        5 pieces of paper (trash)
        candy wrapper
        handful of sand
        twig
        stone
        soda can or cup
        leaf
        soda can flip top

        DO NOT PICK UP GLASS!!!!

When you have found all of the items, turn
around 3 times, shake the hands of one of
the other students, and then go stand
beside your counselor.
```

After the allotted time, the group assembles again. Each shows his collection and discusses whether or not he feels successful.

Some of the ideas which should be explored are:

1. Responsibility can be fun.
2. There are times when one cannot be 100% successful in meeting his responsibilities, and this can be for many reasons.
3. Good effort is the most crucial ingredient in fulfilling responsibility.
4. It <u>feels good</u> to be responsible!

Evaluation

NOTES:

155

SESSION 2

Name Game

Group Discussion

A responsibility I have at school/home...

Materials

Magazines	Glue
Scissors	Piece of large mural paper

Directions

RESPONSIBILITIES COLLAGE

The counselor assigns the group the task of making a collage which shows the many different responsibilities persons have: for themselves, for others, for pets, for property, etc.

The children explain their pictures as they glue them onto the mural. Entitle the mural "Everyone Has Responsibilities".

The students should discuss how many of the pictured responsibilities they actually have.

Evaluation

NOTES:

SESSION 3

Name Game

Group Discussion

My teacher is fair/unfair in assigning classroom responsibilities.

Materials

Copies of Lists of Responsibilities
Copies of Success Cards

Directions

My parents are fair/unfair in assigning home responsibilities.

LIST OF RESPONSIBILITIES

Each student is assigned the task of making two separate lists of his responsibilities at school and at home.

Name _____			
Responsibilities I have at school:	Takes more than 10 minutes	I enjoy doing it	I could have done this 2 yrs. ago
Responsibilities I have at home:			

The older aged children should complete the checklist part of the exercise.

Discuss.

SUCCESS CARDS

Each child should then list a total of five responsibilities on his success card - five which need some improvement. Each day that he fulfills his responsibilities in that area, his teacher or parent should initial the appropriate square.

Instruct each group member to bring his card next session to discuss his progress.

SUCCESS CARD							
Responsibilities	Sun	Mon	Tues	Wed	Thurs	Fri	Sat

Evaluation

NOTES:

SESSION 4

Name Game

Group Discussion

A responsibility I'd like to give away...

Materials

Responsibility, video, 30 minutes
Success Cards

Directions

Review SUCCESS CARDS from last week.

Discuss with each student his degree of success in meeting his responsibilities.

View the video.

Discuss the character's dilemma and possible alternatives. Share experiences where you have been caught in a similar bind.

Discuss why it's important to act responsibly.

Distribute SUCCESS CARDS to be used another week.

Evaluation

NOTES:

SESSION 5

Name Game

**Group
Discussion**

Techniques I used to avoid meeting my responsibilities

Materials

Paper for Bingo Cards   Pens, pencils   Index cards

Directions

Review SUCCESS CARDS from the past week.

Discuss.

RESPONSIBILITY BINGO

Each child chooses his own bingo card. The counselor should go over the symbols and the responsibility each selection denotes.

Making my bed	Going to school
Doing school work	Hanging up clothes
Feeding pets	Wearing clean clothes
Brushing teeth	Treating people with respect
Cleaning my room	Eating the right food
Washing	Cleaning the bathroom
Washing the dishes	Cleaning up around the house
Washing the car	Watching a baby sister or brother
Cleaning the yard	Taking care of materials
Being a good citizen	Clearing the dinner table
Doing homework	Observing safety rules
Earning allowance	

The players take turns picking up a card and making some statement about the responsibility it symbolizes.

EXAMPLE: Taking out the trash is something which should be done each day to help keep a home clean. In my house, it is my brother's responsibility to take out the trash.

Evaluation

SESSION 6

Name Game

Group Discussion

A time when my not meeting my responsibility hurt someone else...

Materials

Recipe on separate index cards
One-cup measuring cup
¼-cup measuring cup
Large spoon
Large mixing bowl

Waxed paper
Small plastic bags
Dish rag and towel
Clean water

Directions

PEANUT BUTTER CANDY MAKING

Ingredients:
    1 cup peanut butter
    1 cup corn syrup
    1¼ cups powdered milk
    1¼ cups powdered sugar

The directions for making the candy are typed on separate index cards. The group members each select a card. Beginning with #1, the student is responsible for carrying out the task written on it. When the activity has been completed, the group should discuss how being a responsible or irresponsible member affects the group's project. Allow each student to evaluate his own efforts.

CARD #1

Instruct the group members to wash their hands.

Set out the following supplies on a <u>clean</u> table.

peanut butter	powdered milk
corn syrup	powdered sugar
measuring cups	mixing bowl
spoon	waxed paper
small plastic bags	

CARD #2

Measure one cup of peanut butter.
Spoon it into the mixing bowl.

CARD #3

Measure one cup of corn syrup.
Pour into the mixing bowl.

CARD #4

Measure 1¼ cups powdered milk.
Pour into the mixing bowl.

CARD #5

Measure 1¼ cups powdered sugar.
Pour into the mixing bowl.

CARD #6

Mix all ingredients together.
Pass bowl to give each person a try at mixing it.

Give each person a sheet of waxed paper and a small plastic bag.

CARD #7

Pour a little bit of powdered sugar on each person's piece of waxed paper.

Divide the peanut butter mixture so that each person gets an equal amount.

CARD #8

Demonstrate rolling a small piece of candy in the powdered sugar. Put it in the plastic bag. Continue until all the peanut butter mixture is used up.

Enlist the help of the group in cleaning all utensils, the table area, and putting supplies away.

Evaluation

NOTES:

ADDITIONAL RESOURCES

Books

Cohen, Shari. *Coping With Failure.*

Holland, R. *About Me*.

Kaufman, G., and Raphael, L. *Stick Up For Yourself*.

Video

You Can Choose! Being Responsible, 25 minutes.
Responsibility, 30 minutes.

School
Behaviors
Group

OBJECTIVES

1. To discuss school rules and the reasons for them.
2. To identify specific appropriate and inappropriate behaviors.
3. To change behavior through an increased understanding of appropriate/ inappropriate behavior.
4. To practice appropriate ways of dealing with rejection.
5. To assume responsibility for one's attitudes, behaviors, and reputation.

Target Group

Ages 6 to 12; 6-10 students per group.

Time Requirement

30-45 minutes per session; 6 sessions.

Whenever you see <u>Name Game</u>, it means:

A simple procedure whereby the first person says, "My name is _____. What is your name?" as she turns to the person on her left. That person says, "My name is _____. Her name is _____. What is your name?" as he turns to the person on his left. And so it goes around the circle.

Whenever you see <u>Evaluation</u>, it means:

At the end of each group session the counselor asks individuals if they feel they have worked toward the goals of the group during that session. The counselor also asks the group members if the individual has done so. There must be a consensus that a person has cooperated and contributed to the group in order for that person to mark his success card with a smiley face.

Students who are disruptive or indifferent may not mark their cards. In the event of a disagreement over the student's eligibility for a smiley face, the counselor has the final say.

This <u>Evaluation</u> activity concludes each session. The counselor may extend it further by setting five smiley faces as a goal for a special reward (pencil, eraser, note pad, discount ticket for a hamburger, etc.)

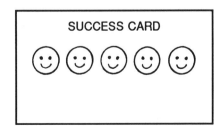

167

SESSION 1

Name Game

Group Discussion

The most difficult school rule for me to follow is...

Materials

How to Conduct Yourself at School, video, 13 minutes
Safety Rules for School, video, 18 minutes

Directions

The counselor shows a video that discusses school rules. Two appropriate videos are: *How to Conduct Yourself at School* and *Safety Rules for School*.

Following the viewing of the videos, discuss <u>reasons</u> for rules.

Make a list of school rules.
Discuss which ones provide for safety.
Discuss which ones are easy/difficult to observe.
Discuss which ones could be eliminated or changed.
Discuss consequences for breaking them.

Evaluation

NOTES:

SESSION 2

Name Game

Group Discussion

When I see someone else breaking a school rule, I...

Materials

12 x 18 white drawing paper
Crayons
Markers

Directions

"WANTED" POSTERS ACTIVITY

Each student is to choose one of the school's rules and make up a "wanted" poster for a violator of that rule. Some examples are:

Cussing Carl	Fighting Freddie
Running Rita	Food Throwing Tessie
Gum Chewing Charlie	Interrupting Ida
Pencil Fighting Peter	Sassy Sam
Smoking Sally	Truant Thomas

The poster should include the name, a picture, information about the inappropriate behavior, and a reward. It should not include the name of a real person.

EXAMPLE: Food Throwing Tessie last seen in lunchroom armed with cornbread in each hand. Considered ill-mannered and undesirable. Reward: $100.

Display the posters around the school.

Evaluation

NOTES:

SESSION 3

Name Game

Group Discussion

What does this quote mean? "If you are not part of the solution, you must be part of the problem."

Materials

None.

Directions

INTERVIEW ACTIVITY

Each student is assigned a staff member and a student safety patrol to interview about school rules and student behavior. The group should brainstorm a few questions which the interviewer might ask. Some possibilities are:

1. What do you consider to be the most frequently violated school rule?
2. In general, how would you describe the behavior of the children in this school?
3. If you were a visitor in this school what would you notice about our students' behavior?
4. What consequences do you consider to be fair for breaking school rules?

The students go out and interview their identified interviewees and then return to the group to discuss the responses they received. The group tries to draw some general conclusions from their responses.

As citizens of this school, the students then make some suggestions as to what their responsibilities are.

Evaluation

NOTES:

SESSION 4

Name Game

**Group
Discussion**

Something I've done which made me disappointed in myself.

Materials

Index Cards: Causes of behaviors and Specific behaviors

Directions

CAUSES OF BEHAVIOR ACTIVITY

The group members divide a group of cards on which each is written
a cause of behavior. Some examples are:

Would like to be stronger	Doesn't know how to do something
Not sure of himself	Doesn't think much of himself
Doesn't want to work	Is worried about home problems
Feels he doesn't belong	Doesn't think people will notice him
Is afraid of failure	Doesn't want to do something
Feels unliked	

The counselor then selects a card from a second group of cards which
describes specific behaviors. Some examples are:

Cries easily	Always tries to be first
Acts afraid	Pushes people around
Acts shy	Acts silly
Shows off	Acts tired
Complains of illness	Is loud

The students must then match the cause with the behavior. There
are no right or wrong answers. Much discussion can be stimulated
as to an individual's reasoning behind his or her choices. Relate
personal experiences.

Discuss the idea that we do not always know <u>why</u> we act as we do.
And that sometimes we are not very pleased with ourselves for what
we have done. Nevertheless, we are still OK people.

Evaluation

NOTES:

SESSION 5

Name Game

Group Discussion

If I were in charge of this school...

Materials

None.

Directions

WELCOME BACK ACTIVITY

One student volunteers to be away from the group. The group forms a circle. A hypothetical discussion proceeds as to why the student has been rejected from the group. The student is invited to return to the room. The "rejected" student suggests an inappropriate behavior which he pretends to have done as the reason for his having been ostracized from the group. If his suggestion is one that the group had discussed, he must suggest an alternative way of behaving, listing specific behaviors.

If his suggestion is not one that the group had discussed, he must guess again.

After completing the task, the student is welcomed back into the circle.

Another student volunteers to be sent away from the group and the activity is repeated.

A discussion follows as to one's feeling over having been excluded from the group and then having been welcomed back.

Emphasize the idea that sometimes we unconsciously ostracize ourselves from a group through out behavior. When we realize this has happened, it becomes necessary to make a conscious effort to modify our behavior.

Evaluation

NOTES:

SESSION 6

Name Game

Group Discussion

Three feelings I have experienced in school today are...

Materials

Cellophane (red, blue, yellow)
Oaktag
Glue
Eyeglasses

Directions

ATTITUDE GLASSES ACTIVITY

Discuss <u>attitude</u> and how your attitude toward things and people affects how you feel about them and sometimes how you act.

The counselor introduces the yellow or "sunny" attitude glasses, puts them on, and exclaims, "My, what a beautiful group of students you are! You always brighten my day!"

She repeats the exercise with the blue, depressing attitude glasses and says, "Oh nuts, you're here again! I am so tired of your problems."

Finally, with the red "angry" attitude glasses, she says "You better be having a good week in your classes because if I hear a bad report, you're going to be sorry!"

The students will hardly be able to wait their turns to try on the different glasses and make comments to fit the mood or attitude of the lens color.

If time allows, allow students to make their own glasses to take with them.

Discuss how our comments affect our feelings and those of others. Emphasize that much of how we view school life and how others view us is within our control.

Evaluation

NOTES:

ADDITIONAL RESOURCES

Books

Holland, R. *About Me*.

Scott, Sharon. *How to Say No and Keep Your Friends.*

Wirths, C. & Kruhm, M. *I Hate School.*

Videos

How to Conduct Yourself at School, 13 minutes.

Safety Rules for School, 18 minutes.

Self-Concept Group

OBJECTIVES

1. To recognize and express one's own feelings.
2. To identify one's strengths and weaknesses.
3. To feel good about one's self.
4. To participate in activities which emphasize the uniqueness of one's self.
5. To communicate with others positive perceptions of one's self.
6. To communicate to others positive perceptions of them.

Target Group

Ages 6 to 8; 6-10 children per group.

Time Requirement

30-40 minutes per session; 6 sessions.

Target Group

Ages 9 to 12; 6-10 children per group.

Time Requirement

45 minutes per session; 6 sessions.

Whenever you see Name Game, it means:

A simple procedure whereby the first person says, "My name is _____. What is your name?" as she turns to the person on her left. That person says, "My name is _____ _____. Her name is _____. What is your name?" as he turns to the person on his left. And so it goes around the circle.

Whenever you see Evaluation, it means:

At the end of each group session the counselor asks individuals if they feel they have worked toward the goals of the group during that session. The counselor also asks the group members if the individual has done so. There must be a consensus that a person has cooperated and contributed to the group in order for that person to mark his success card with a smiley face.

Students who are disruptive or indifferent may not mark their cards. In the event of a disagreement over the student's eligibility for a smiley face, the counselor has the final say.

This Evaluation activity concludes each session. The counselor may extend it further by setting five smiley faces as a goal for a special reward (pencil, eraser, note pad, discount ticket for a hamburger, etc.)

SESSION 1 Ages 6 to 8

Name Game

**Group
Discussion**

Today I feel...

Materials

Hand puppets

Directions

PUPPET TALK ACTIVITY

Each group member is invited to introduce himself to the group by using a puppet. He might share his favorite color, favorite food, brothers' or sisters' names, what he likes to do, how he feels about school, etc.

After each person finishes, the group applauds him.

Next, the students use the puppets to ask each other questions.

Evaluation

NOTES:

SESSION 2 Ages 6 to 8

Name Game

Group Discussion

Today I feel good about...
Today I don't feel very good about...

Materials

Full-length mirror   Scissors
White Butcher paper   Crayons or markers

Directions

MIRROR MESSAGE ACTIVITY

Each child walks up to a full-length mirror, looks himself over carefully, and completes this sentence: "When I look in the mirror, I feel good about..."

BODY DRAWING

Each student is invited to lie down on a pre-cut sheet of paper and assume any pose he chooses. The counselor traces each child's outline. Each child must then draw and color his features, clothes, etc. The child cuts it out and the counselor hangs it on the wall.

Discuss the uniqueness of each individual.

Evaluation

NOTES:

SESSION 3 Ages 6 to 8

Name Game

Group Discussion

I like myself because...

Materials

Patches of fuzzy material
Pipe cleaners
Movable eyes
Construction paper
Glue
Scissors
Safety pins

Directions

Explain that a fuzzy is a good deed or act. Discuss how giving a fuzzy away is contagious and name persons to whom they might give a fuzzy. Discuss the different kinds of fuzzies which can be exchanged (smiles, favors, good school work).

The children make two warm fuzzies out of the materials provided: one is to wear and one is to give away to a friend. When the child gives his fuzzy away, he should tell the person what he likes about him.

Evaluation

NOTES:

SESSION 4 Ages 6 to 8

Name Game

Group Discussion

If I could change one thing about myself...

Materials

1 piece 12 x 18 white construction paper/child
Scissors   Hole puncher
Yarn   Beanbags
Crayons or Markers   Feelings wheel

Directions

FEELINGS WHEEL ACTIVITY

Each student throws the beanbag onto the feelings wheel, which is lying on the floor. Whatever feeling word the beanbag lands on, the child tells a time when he felt that way. If it lands on more than one, the child may choose which one to discuss.

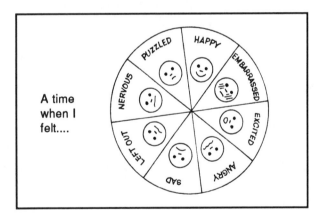

FEELINGS NECKLACES ACTIVITY

The students cut circles about 2½ inches in diameter out of the white paper. The counselor punches 1 hole at the top of each circle. The child draws a different feeling face (which shows some of the feelings he has) on each circle. The student threads the circles with yarn and ties it around his neck.

Evaluation

NOTES:

181

Name Game

Group Discussion

Something I could teach someone else to do is...

Materials

None.

Directions

ROLE PLAY ACTIVITY

Each child has an opportunity to role play each of the following topics, one at a time.

Something I do well
Something I like to do
Something that scares me
Something that I do every summer
Something I like to do with my friend
Something I like to do alone

The group members must guess what the individual is role playing.

Discuss each person's <u>uniqueness</u>.

TENDER TOUCH ACTIVITY

The group lines up one behind the other. One person walks past the group very slowly. As he passes each person, that person touches the one walking by and says something positive to him or about him.

Evaluation

NOTES:

SESSION 6 Ages 6 to 8

Name Game

Group Discussion

Someday I'll be famous for...

Materials

Yellow construction paper (Two 9 x 12 sheets/child)
Cardboard star pattern
Polaroid camera (optional)
Fine-tip markers
Glue
Yarn
Paper punch

Directions

YOU ARE A STAR!

Each child traces the star pattern on one piece of construction paper. Cut star shape out double so you have two stars. Paste the two stars together. Punch a hole in the top and string a piece of yarn through it.

The counselor takes a polaroid snapshot of 2 or 3 children together, standing with some space between them. The counselor cuts around the individual persons and gives each child his own picture. The child glues his photograph to one side of the star and writes his name under it. If no camera is available, the child draws his own picture on the star.

Each child turns the star over to the back side and writes something positive about himself.

The star is then passed around the circle. Each group member writes something positive on the star. Each child takes his star with him to hang in the classroom or at home.

Evaluation

NOTES:

183

SESSION 1 Ages 9 to 12

Name Game

Group Discussion

Things people can see about me...

Materials

Bread - one slice per child
Peanut butter
Knife
Raisins

Peanuts
Chow mein noodles
Coconut
Waxed paper

Directions

Divide the group into pairs. Instruct the students to carry on a normal conversation for five minutes, each person telling another as much as possible about himself. The students should pick those things about themselves which they consider to be important to share. After a few minutes, the group returns to the circle. Each student introduces his partner to the group by telling a few things about him.

PEANUT BUTTER FACES ACTIVITY

Each group member spreads peanut butter on bread and then uses the additional ingredients to make a face which shows how he is feeling right now. Share with the group. The students should be encouraged to elaborate on why they feel that way.

Evaluation

NOTES:

SESSION 2 Ages 9 to 12

Name Game

Group Discussion

Things I do well...

Materials

One sheet 9 x 12 construction paper per child
Newspaper
Clear tape or white glue
Photo face of each child
Masking tape or double-faced tape
Crayons or colored felt-tipped pens

Directions

The students are asked to share 2 or 3 things at which they feel they have been successful.

ME IN THE SCHOOL PAPER ACTIVITY

Discuss the types of services which are advertised in the newspaper. Look at an ad and discuss the kinds of information in it.

Each child must choose a service or product to advertise which he could offer realistically. The child may write one on plant-sitting, dog-walking, baking, letter-writing, or toy-swapping services. Or the student can advertise a product for sale such as plants he has raised, hand-crafted objects, etc.

Next, the child must design the ad, using his photo and information about him and his service.

If your school prints a newspaper, inquire about including these in the next issue.

Evaluation

NOTES:

SESSION 3 Ages 9 to 12

Name Game

Group Discussion

FEELING WORDS

Materials

Feelings Words ditto
One 12 x 18 sheet black construction paper/student
White chalk   Glue   Scissors

Directions

FEELINGS WORDS ACTIVITY

Each group member circles the feelings words on a given ditto sheet - words which describe him.

The counselor helps to trace the silhouettes of each group member on black construction paper. The student cuts out his silhouette and the words which he circled. He glues the words which describe himself onto the silhouette.

The students share five to eight of the words they've chosen with the group. The silhouettes are displayed in the counselor's room.

Feeling Words Work Sheet:

ANGRY	APPRECIATIVE	ANNOYED	ANXIOUS
ASTONISHED	ASHAMED	BORED	CONTENTED
CRITICAL	CHEERFUL	DEPRESSED	DISGUSTED
DISSATISFIED	DISCOURAGED	DISAPPOINTED	EAGER
DELIGHTED	ENVIOUS	EXCITED	GUILTY
ENCOURAGED	EMBARRASSED	FRUSTRATED	GRUMPY
GLOOMY	HAPPY	HATEFUL	IRRITATED
INDIFFERENT	INTERESTED	JEALOUS	LOVING
MISERABLE	PROUD	PLEASED	RESTLESS
RELAXED	SILLY	SAD	SCARED
SURPRISED	SATISFIED	TENSE	TIRED

SESSION 3 Ages 9 to 12 continued

Evaluation

NOTES:

SESSION 4 Ages 9 to 12

Name Game

Group Discussion

I made someone feel great/awful when...

Materials

Drawing paper   Scissors
Crayons   *IALAC*, video

Directions

IALAC ACTIVITY

The students make IALAC tags out of drawing paper and crayons. The students view the video *IALAC*. As each put-down is heard in the filmstrip, the students tear a piece of their IALAC tags away.

Following the filmstrip, the students discuss how put-downs feel, what put-downs they're likely to give and receive, and why people use put-downs.

TENDER TOUCH ACTIVITY

(Refer to Session 5 - Ages 6 to 8, SELF-CONCEPT).

Evaluation

NOTES:

Name Game

Group Discussion

A time I wish I had stood up for my rights.

Materials

None.

Directions

Discuss ASSERTIVENESS as a technique to express one's thoughts and feelings honestly and forthrightly without putting another person down. Assertiveness helps identify the problem and specifically clarify one's position.

Introduce the I-message format:

When you _____,
            (Offensive behavior)

I feel _____
            (Feeling word)

because _____.
            (Effect of behavior)

Provide some examples of I-messages and then practice using I-messages in the given situations.

EXAMPLE: When you fail my tests because you haven't studied, I feel disappointed because it seems I'm wasting my time trying to teach you.

EXAMPLE: When you load us down with homework on weekends, I feel discouraged because I never seem to have time to do other things I really enjoy.

SITUATIONS:

1. Mary Ellen is doing her homework. Her brother has the TV turned up so loud she can't concentrate.

2. Jack wants to borrow lunch money from Fred for the third day in a row. He knows Fred always has extra money on him because he works after school.

189

3. Beth has enjoyed having Sharon for her friend but lately Sharon has begun hanging around with a crowd that has a reputation for drinking. Beth knows she doesn't want to get involved.

4. Mrs. Albright is a very nice neighbor but her dog, Rags, barked all night long, keeping Jim's family up.

5. Chris' doctor put her on a strict diet because she is overweight. Her mother sends her to school with what she is supposed to eat but Chris begs you at lunch to share some of your lunch with her because she is so hungry.

6. Your dad says you must get a haircut. You agree but want it cut in a style that is flattering to your face. Your dad says you must get a military cut because that's what he wore as a boy.

7. You spend the night at a friend's house with several of your friends. One of the kids brought cigarettes. She dares everyone to try one. Everyone does. Now it's your turn.

8. You got your test paper back and your grade is a D. After looking it over, you see two answers which were incorrectly marked wrong. You tell your teacher but she says it's obvious to her that you changed the answers.

9. Jermaine is a kid who always has something smart to say. No one takes him very seriously. Today, he has begun making fun of your mother and it is getting on your nerves.

10. The teacher has announced that tryouts for the school play will take place next week. She has scheduled several of your classmates to try out but hasn't asked you. You think you'd like to give it a try too.

Summarize the purpose of I-messages.

Encourage the students to suggest other appropriate uses of I-messages.

Evaluation

NOTES:

190

SESSION 6 Ages 9 to 12

Name Game

Group Discussion

I am lovable and capable because...

Materials

Chips or coins (100 per student)
List of sale items

Directions

VALUES SALE ACTIVITY

Provide each student with 100 chips. Announce that the students will have an opportunity to buy some items with their money, but in order to do so, they will have to out-bid everyone else.

Provide each student with a list of items up for sale.

1. love	11. kindness
2. fame	12. competitiveness
3. $1,000,000	13. good grades
4. intelligence	14. stereo
5. bravery	15. happiness
6. revenge	16. sense of humor
7. family harmony	17. athletic ability
8. friends	18. peace
9. honesty	19. own telephone
10. good looks	20. career

Allow them time to prioritize the items they wish to bid on and the amounts they wish to bid.

Introduce one item at a time. Listen to the bids. Award the item (a card with the item name written on it) to the highest bidder in exchange for the corresponding number of chips. Continue until items for bid or chips are exhausted.

Conclude with a discussion of their values. Did an individual choose tangibles/intangibles; something they need/something they want; something someone else wants for you?

Conclude with I learned... statements. Each member has the opportunity to tell one thing he learned while being in the group today - about himself or someone else, or just about being in the group.

SESSION 6 Ages 9 to 12 continued

Evaluation

NOTES:

ADDITIONAL RESOURCES

Books

Crary, E. *My Name is Not Dummy.*

Crary, E. *Let's Talk About Feelings.*

Holland, R. *About Me*.

Kaufman, G., & Raphael, L. *Stick Up For Yourself.*

Videos

You Can Choose! Being Responsible, 25 minutes.

Self-Esteem, 15 minutes.

You Are Special, 30 minutes.

Other Materials

Hand Puppets (Family).

Shyness Group

OBJECTIVES

1. To provide a safe environment where group members will speak out about themselves and their worlds.
2. To encourage interaction among peers.
3. To become more aware of one's physical being through a sensory approach.
4. To identify one's feelings and strengths.
5. To role play ways of handling difficult situations.

Target Group

Ages 6 to 8; 6-10 children per group.

Time Requirement

30 minutes per session; 6 sessions.

Target Group

Ages 9 to 12; 6-10 children per group.

Time Requirement

45 minutes per session; 6 sessions.

Whenever you see Name Game, it means:

A simple procedure whereby the first person says, "My name is _____. What is your name?" as she turns to the person on her left. That person says, "My name is _____ _____. Her name is _____. What is your name?" as he turns to the person on his left. And so it goes around the circle.

Whenever you see Evaluation, it means:

At the end of each group session the counselor asks individuals if they feel they have worked toward the goals of the group during that session. The counselor also asks the group members if the individual has done so. There must be a consensus that a person has cooperated and contributed to the group in order for that person to mark his success card with a smiley face.

Students who are disruptive or indifferent may not mark their cards. In the event of a disagreement over the student's eligibility for a smiley face, the counselor has the final say.

This Evaluation activity concludes each session. The counselor may extend it further by setting five smiley faces as a goal for a special reward (pencil, eraser, note pad, discount ticket for a hamburger, etc.)

197

SESSION 1 Ages 6 to 8

Name Game

**Group
Discussion**

Given a face puppet, each group member will hold it in front of his face and tell the group three things about himself.

Materials

Chocolate pudding   Finger painting paper
Milk   Water
Measuring cup

Directions

FINGER PAINTING WITH PUDDING ACTIVITY

The students should wash their hands thoroughly. Using chocolate pudding, each student will finger paint his self-portrait and name on his finger painting paper. Children are encouraged to lick their fingers if they so desire.

The dried paintings are displayed on the walls. The children are encouraged to talk among themselves as they ooze their way through their paintings.

To wrap up, have each group member complete the sentence: "Right now, I feel..."

Evaluation

NOTES:

SESSION 2 Ages 6 to 8

Name Game

Group Discussion

It's difficult for me to...
It's easy for me to...

Materials

Twister game

Directions

TWISTER

The children play the game Twister. Interaction is encouraged as the children slip and slide and fall through the game.

The counselor takes a group photograph, mounts it on a piece of construction paper, labels it "Our Group", and hangs it in the counselor's room. Each group member signs his name on the paper.

Evaluation

NOTES:

SESSION 3 Ages 6 to 8

Name Game

Group Discussion

The way I feel most often is...

Materials

Feelings Blocks game board
One beanbag
Pieces of fruit
Crayons

Directions

FEELINGS FRUIT

Each group member receives an orange (apple, pear) and with a crayon draws a face showing his feeling. After the faces have been shared, the group uses the back side of the orange to show their favorite feelings.

FEELINGS BLOCKS

Each student throws the beanbag on the game board. The student tells about a time when he had that feeling.

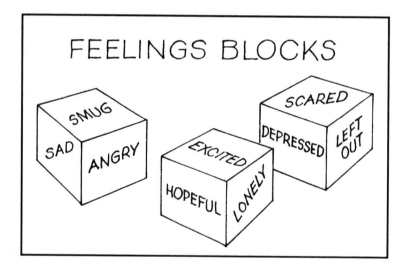

Evaluation

NOTES:

SESSION 4 Ages 6 to 8

Name Game

Group Discussion

I get nervous...
I get excited when...

Materials

Cardboard mirror patterns   Glue
Dittos of Magic Mirror poem   Oaktag
Mirror film or aluminum foil

Directions

MAGIC MIRROR

Each child traces and cuts a mirror shape from oaktag. He glues mirror film or aluminum foil over the top of one side and trims around the edges.

The counselor and the group read the poem, discuss it, and glue it to the other side of the mirror.

Each group member tells what feelings he thinks his magic mirror would see inside of him.

MY MAGIC MIRROR

My magic mirror sees deep inside
All the things I sometimes hide.
The way I think, and see, and feel,
My magic mirror will reveal.
The things I want to do or be
Are all a special part of me.
That other folks will never know,
For outwardly they hardly show.
But I can tell you what you'd see
If you looked in my mirror with me.

201

SESSION 4 Ages 6 to 8 continued

Evaluation

NOTES:

SESSION 5 Ages 6 to 8

Name Game

Group Discussion

Thinking of snakes makes me...
Thinking of ice cream makes me...

Materials

Strips of paper with role plays

Directions

ROLE PLAY

Each student draws a situation strip of paper out of a container. The counselor helps the child read and understand it. The student can select a buddy or buddies to help role play the situation.

The rest of the group must identify the problem and tell their reaction to the role player's enacted solution. The group applauds for the role players when they finish.

Some sample role plays are:

1. Mary is new in school. She doesn't have any friends. To cover up her shyness, Mary pretends she doesn't care. She even criticizes her new school, its teachers and students. One teacher, however, has let Mary know that she understands how hard it is to be the new kid in school and that she is willing to help Mary make the adjustment. Mary finally decides to go to the teacher and ask for help.

2. Steve has been studying hard for his math test. Two of his friends have laughed at him, telling him they know how to make good grades without studying. Following the test, Mrs. Sims, the teacher, tells the class that she has reason to believe that some of her students have cheated. Unless someone comes forward and tells the truth, everyone will receive an F. Steve is very upset. He got an A on the test. He <u>thinks</u> his friends were the ones who cheated, but he has no proof. If he tells, he fears he will lose their friendship. If he doesn't he feels he'll be dishonest and he'll lose the A he worked so hard to get.

3. John's baby sister, Jennifer, is only 3 years old. John loves her and she adores John but sometimes she can be a pain. John's friends have told him they are tired of Jennifer tagging along all the time. John's mother is divorced and she really needs John to help her babysit Jennifer while she tries to take care of the house, shop, etc. John wants to help his mother but he

doesn't want to lose his friends either. This Saturday, John and his friends have made plans to fly kites in the field next to John's house. John's mother has just said, "John, I have a lot to do this Saturday to get ready for Grandma's visit on Sunday so I hope I can count on you to watch Jennifer for me."

4. Mrs. Love is Kathy's teacher. Mrs. Love thinks Kathy is the most precious child she has ever taught. She picks Kathy for almost every special job, privilege, etc. The other students have begun to notice and to tease her about being Mrs. Love's pet. Although Kathy likes having the special attention from Mrs. Love, she is worried about losing her friends.

5. Ellen is a quiet little girl whom most people do not notice. She would like to have a lot of friends but doesn't know how to go about getting people to notice her. One day much to Ellen's surprise, Barbara who has lots of friends asked Ellen if she could borrow her pencil. Ellen gave it to her. Barbara didn't return it at the end of the day, but Ellen didn't mind. She was glad that Barbara had even noticed her. Over the next few days, Barbara asked to borrow Ellen's lunch money, paper, candy, and finally, her homework. Ellen was torn between the feelings of wanting to be accepted and fear of being used.

6. Bobby was selected by his Cub Scout leader to welcome the parents at the next meeting. He and his mother wrote his speech. He practiced and practiced, even saying it to himself in front of the mirror. But as the day of the meeting drew nearer, Bobby began to doubt that he could do it. He thought he might even get sick if he tried.

Evaluation

NOTES:

SESSION 6 Ages 6 to 8

Name Game

Group Discussion

When I first joined this group, I felt...
Now I feel...

Materials

None.

Directions

Compare <u>then</u> and <u>now</u> feelings.

Discuss why there might have been a change.

BODY GAMES - Sensory Awareness

1. Rag Doll-Tin Soldier
   Students pair up. In the first round, A's will be tin soldiers and B's will be their directors. Tin soldiers can only move forward. They have no power to think or make decisions. A tin soldier walks slowly with stiff legs and arm joints. B's job is to guide his tin soldier and to turn him so as to avoid hitting walls, tables, and other tin soldiers walking around the room.

   After a few minutes, reverse roles and do it again.

   Encourage students to verbalize their reactions to the exercise.

2. Human Pretzel
   Send one person out of the group. This person becomes the detective. The rest of the group joins hands in a circle. Then without breaking the hand contact, they tangle themselves up by going under, over, in and out of each other's arms. When the group is thoroughly entangled, ask the detective to return and try to untangle the group by giving verbal instructions to different people as to how they should move.

3. Mirroring
   The group stands in two rows, facing the same way. The students in the front row begin to move their whole bodies, including their arms and their legs. Have the students in the back row try to exactly copy every move of the student directly in front of him.

   Reverse positions and repeat.

   Explain to the students that this is called "mirroring". Talk about what happens when we look into a real mirror.

SESSION 6   Ages 6 to 8 continued

Now have the students face each other. Have one be the "mirror", the one who copies exactly, and the other the "doer", the one who controls the mirror's actions.

Reverse roles and repeat.

Encourage the students to use their whole bodies, including facial expressions.

Discuss whether leading or following was easier for each person.

Evaluation

NOTES:

100 Ways to Enhance Self-Concept in the Classroom by Jack Canfield, Prentice-Hall Englewood Cliffs, New Jersey, 1976, p. 150-151. Reprinted by permission of Prentice-Hall, Inc., Englewood Cliffs, NJ.

SESSION 1 Ages 9 to 12

Name Game

Group Discussion

What I like best/least about myself.

Materials

Finger painting paper
Finger paint

Directions

FINGER PAINTING FEELINGS ACTIVITY

The students will be given an opportunity to finger paint their names and surround them with feelings words which describe themselves.

Share completed paintings with the group.

If students experience a reluctance to begin the finger painting activity, allow time to discuss that reluctance and the reasons for it.

Evaluation

NOTES:

SESSION 2 Ages 9 to 12

Name Game

Group Discussion

A time I made someone proud of me.

Materials

Copies of Feelings Bingo Cards
Individual Feelings Cards

Directions

FEELINGS BINGO

Each group member chooses a card with feelings words randomly positioned on it. In turn, each person pulls a feelings card, reads the feeling word, tells a time when he felt that way. Each person in the group covers the word on his game card. The first person to get a row or column covered calls "BINGO."

Sample Card

sad	happy	surprised	tired
dependable	embarrassed	excited	dejected
angry	neglected	hungry	ecstatic
anxious	left-out	hurt	depressed

Evaluation

NOTES:

SESSION 3 Ages 9 to 12

Name Game

Group Discussion

Something I find difficult to do before a group.

Materials

Strips of paper with role plays

Directions

WHAT TO DO? - Role Play

Each group member will have the opportunity to pull and read one of the "situation" strips of paper. The student may pick a partner to help the role play. Some examples of situations might be:

1. a shy person who must give an oral report to the class
2. a babysitter who encounters a parent who refuses to leave a number where she can be reached
3. classmates who are making fun of a new boy in school

Additional role plays are available in Session #5 - Ages 6 to 8 of the Shyness Group.

The role players have 3 minutes to act out the situation and their solution.

The rest of the group then tries to identify the enacted solution to the problem. They offer alternate solutions and discuss the value of each.

The group discusses the relevance of the situations to the members' lives.

Evaluation

NOTES:

SESSION 4 Ages 9 to 12

Name Game

Group Discussion

If I could be a famous person, I would want to be...

Materials

Copies of worksheet

Directions

ASSERTIVENESS

The counselor discusses with the group the principles of assertion; the difference between assertion and aggression. Assertiveness can be viewed as expressing one's thoughts and feelings honestly and forthrightly without putting another person down. Aggression is accusing, striking out, blaming. Assertiveness when used appropriately can clarify a situation and allow for a possible solution. Aggression almost always creates anger or defensiveness which denies any constructive outcome.

Given the following work sheet, allow the group members to label the statements as assertive or aggressive. Discuss the statements as a group. Encourage the group to create some statements on their own.

WORK SHEET

Label the following statements as ASSERTIVE (AS) or AGGRESSIVE (AG).

1. You're always picking on me!

2. If you and dad weren't such slobs, I wouldn't be either.

3. I feel threatened when you watch over my shoulder like that.

4. You'll do what I say and you'll do it now.

5. I will be leaving at 10:00 and if your homework is done, you may go with me.

6. Mrs. Johnson, when you give an assignment, it would be helpful to me if you would write it on the board.

7. That's too much work! She's crazy if she thinks I'm going to do it!

8. When I see you talking and laughing with Julie and Kim, sometimes I wonder if you're laughing at me.

9. It makes me upset when you and daddy argue in front of me.

10. Get out of the way, Punk! I'm coming through!

SESSION 4 Ages 9 to 12 continued

Evaluation

NOTES:

SESSION 5 Ages 9 to 12

Name Game

Group Discussion

My goal in life.

Materials

Writing paper   Pens, pencils

Directions

Review the discussion of assertiveness and aggressiveness. Ask the group to identify examples of each which they have witnessed during the past week.

Present I-messages as a way of making assertive statements.

Use the form:

When _____
            (Identify offending behavior)

it makes me feel _____
                    (Identify feeling word)

because _____.
            (Identify effect of behavior)

EXAMPLE: Parents want their child's stereo turned down.

I-message: When you play the stereo so loud, it makes me feel angry because I can't enjoy the book I'm trying to read.

Challenge the students to write I-messages for each of the following situations.

1. Just after Judy's mother finished cleaning, Judy and her friends sat in front of the TV eating potato chips and pretzels.

2. Mr. Cooper surprises his class with a math quiz today and some of the students are upset.

3. Mrs. Smiley compares her son who is an average student to his sister who gets straight A's.

4. Mr. Wilder's newspaper was sitting in a puddle of water in his front yard this morning.

5. Tommy keeps telling his friend, "If you'd just try harder, I know you could win. You're not trying!"

6. Jean goes to dance lessons, scouts, and her church group meetings. Her personal time is very limited. Now her mother wants her to take piano lessons too.

7. Gerry's friends call him "chicken" because he won't smoke with them.

8. Mrs. Coate's dog chases the kids in the neighborhood when they go past his yard. Today, he caused Annie to fall down and skin her knee.

9. The teacher had just told the class that they may not go outside for P.E. because some of the students misbehaved in the lunchroom.

10. Mrs. Thatcher constantly criticizes her son, Benny, because she wants him to try always to do better.

Encourage the students to name other relevant situations where I-messages might be used effectively.

Evaluation

NOTES:

SESSION 6 Ages 9 to 12

Name Game

Group Discussion

A situation in which I used an I-message this past week (or wish I had).

Materials

Puppets
Choice of children's stories

Directions

PUPPET PLAY

Using puppets and a script prepared from an easy children's book, allow students to read through it a couple of times. Emphasize voice projection and animation. Encourage the students to <u>be</u> their puppets.

Arrange to have a Kindergarten class come in to view the puppet play.

Ask each puppeteer to introduce himself and his puppet to the class. Encourage applause from the audience. Encourage the audience to ask questions of the puppets which the puppeteers will answer.

Evaluation

NOTES:

ADDITIONAL RESOURCES

<u>Books</u>

Crary, Elizabeth. *Let's Talk About Feelings.*

Holland, R. *About Me*.

Kaufman, G. & Raphael, L. *Stick Up For Yourself.*

Polland, Ph.D., Barbara. *Feelings Inside You, and Out Loud, Too.*

Scott, Sharon. *When to Say Yes and Make More Friends.*

<u>Game</u>

Twister.

Study Skills & Work Habits Group

OBJECTIVES

1. To identify specific behaviors which develop good work and study habits.
2. To organize time more effectively with regard to task completion.
3. To examine one's current use of time.
4. To make a slide/tape presentation of good study skills/work habits.

Target Group

Ages 9 to 12; 6-10 students per group.

Time Requirement

45 minutes per session; 7 sessions.

Whenever you see Name Game, it means:

A simple procedure whereby the first person says, "My name is _____. What is your name?" as she turns to the person on her left. That person says, "My name is _____. Her name is _____. What is your name?" as he turns to the person on his left. And so it goes around the circle.

Whenever you see Evaluation, it means:

At the end of each group session the counselor asks individuals if they feel they have worked toward the goals of the group during that session. The counselor also asks the group members if the individual has done so. There must be a consensus that a person has cooperated and contributed to the group in order for that person to mark his success card with a smiley face.

Students who are disruptive or indifferent may not mark their cards. In the event of a disagreement over the student's eligibility for a smiley face, the counselor has the final say.

This Evaluation activity concludes each session. The counselor may extend it further by setting five smiley faces as a goal for a special reward (pencil, eraser, note pad, discount ticket for a hamburger, etc.)

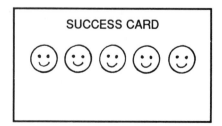

219

SESSION 1

Name Game

Group Discussion

My strengths are...
My weaknesses are...

Materials

None.

Directions

FOLLOWING DIRECTIONS/LISTENING ACTIVITY

The group of students structures a runway of chairs or people, wide enough for a person to walk the length. Litter the runway with books and pencils. The group then selects one person who is to be blindfolded to be the pilot. Another person is to play the part of the control tower. He can station himself anywhere he desires for maximum visibility. A storm has hit - lightning has knocked out the transmitter of the plane, although the receiver is still working. The pilot can receive but can't send messages. The control tower must help the pilot land the plane without damage by sending directions over the radio. If the pilot brushes against any object on the runway the plane sustains damage. Total incidents of damage are recorded for each pilot.

Compare through discussion how piloting a plane without being able to see or ask directions is like trying to succeed in academics without good study skills and work habits. Allow the pilots to express their frustrations at feeling lost and doomed to failure.

Repeat the exercise several times without the blindfold and with two-way communication between pilot and control tower. Discuss the differences in rate of success (absence of damage), pilot's feelings, need for outside support, etc.

Reinforce the essential need of good study skills and work habits for the student who is attempting to pilot his way through school. Point out that following directions and listening are two essential skills.

Evaluation

NOTES:

SESSION 2

Name Game

Group Discussion

If my teacher could change one thing about me, it would be...

Materials

Chart paper	Camera
Markers	Copies of "test"

Directions

TEST ACTIVITY

The students will take a "test" given by the counselor.

Name _____

DIRECTIONS: Read all the questions on the page before you begin
answering them.

1. What is your full name?

2. What is your address?

3. When was the last time you ate chicken?

4. What is the capital of Georgia?

5. When is your birthday?

6. What is your favorite song?

7. Who is the president of the U.S.?

8. Do not do questions 1 - 7. Sign your name at the bottom of the paper.
   Put your pencil down. Turn your paper over. Sit quietly and see how
   many others followed the directions.

Following activity, discuss the purpose of such an exercise. Discuss the importance of following directions.

Brainstorm as many good work habits and study habits as possible. Make a list for the group to read. Some examples might be:

1. Have a clean lighted area in which to work.
2. Schedule yourself adequate uninterrupted time in which to get the job done.

221

3. Get enough rest and eat properly.
4. Get materials ready before you begin - sharpen pencils, get paper, books, etc.
5. Avoid outside disturbances (radio, TV, brothers, sisters, etc.).
6. Use available resources.
7. Ask appropriate persons for help when necessary.
8. Proofread your work.
9. Take pride in your work.
10. Listen carefully to directions.
11. Raise your hand to get the teacher's attention.
12. Participate in group work when it is advantageous and appropriate.

FILMING SCHEDULE

As a group, set up a picture-taking schedule so that two group members at a time will go with the counselor to "catch" students in other classes on film displaying good work and study habits. Follow the schedule during the week.

Evaluation

NOTES:

SESSION 3

Name Game

**Group
Discussion**

The greatest sense of accomplishment I have ever felt was when...

Materials

Poster board
Photos from previous week

Directions

Allow students time to discuss their experiences while taking photos last week. View the photographs. Allow the group to arrange them on poster board and write the captions.

Display the poster in a prominent area with the group members' names credited.

Evaluation

NOTES:

SESSION 4

Name Game

Group Discussion

I find I spend too much time on... and not enough time on...

Materials

Writing paper
Pens, pencils

Directions

TIME MANAGEMENT ACTIVITY

List as a group the kinds of obstacles which prevent you from getting things finished in the time that you have.

Some examples might be: getting unexpected chores assigned, wasting time, daydreaming, over-scheduling, unexpected delays, little brother/sister gets in the way.

Discuss which of these things are under one's control and which are not.

Each student should make a TIME LINE for one day.

7 AM	8	9	10	11	12 PM	1	2	3	4	5	6	7	8	9	10	11 PM

Write down the name of each activity you usually do during the course of a day.

Do it again for a weekend day.

Discuss how they differ.

Discuss flexible time (time when you can vary what you do). Discuss ways of using it wisely to complete tasks you never seem to have time for.

Evaluation

NOTES:

SESSION 5

Name Game

Group Discussion

I wish I hade more time for...

Materials

Copies of Study Readiness thermometer

Directions

TIME MANAGEMENT: Scheduling Time Effectively

In order to make good use of one's time, one has to know what he wants or needs to accomplish.

Discuss the following ideas with the group:

Write down all assignments, short-term and long-term.
Record due dates on your calendar.
Prioritize your list of things you want/need to do.
Post your list where you can see it.
Cross off each thing as you complete it.
Don't allow yourself to procrastinate.
Don't allow yourself to daydream or get distracted by doing something you prefer.
Do what you say you will do.
Try timing yourself to do things and then improving on that time.
Tell others of your plans and welcome their reminding you.
Reward yourself for completing assignments.

Provide each student with a Study Readiness Thermometer. Provide time to do each task and then record his progress on the thermometer.

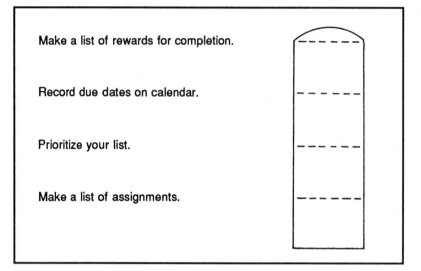

Evaluation

NOTES:

SESSION 6

Name Game

Group Discussion

I think tests are...

Materials

None.

Directions

TEST TAKING DISCUSSION

Discuss the importance of taking tests, the reasons for them, and some ideas for preparing for them. Some suggestions which may need to be reviewed:

Get plenty of rest.
Eat a balanced breakfast.
Avoid arguments at home and on the bus prior to testing.
Come to school with the necessary supplies to take the test.

When studying:

Try to guess which questions will be on the test.
Review chapter headings.
Tell someone what you have read.
Review end-of-chapter questions.
Summarize chapter contents.
Review class notes.
Reread parts of the book which are not clear.

During the test:

Relax - practice deep breaths, tensing and relaxing muscles.
Read questions twice.
Don't spend too much time on any one question.
Check over your answers.

After the test:

Read the teacher's comments carefully so you don't make the same mistake twice.

Conclude this session with a Critical Thinking Activity:

Given information: John and Mary are on the floor. There is water and broken glass on the floor. Mary is dead. What happened?

The students ask questions. The counselor may answer only "yes", "no", or "does not compute".

ANSWER: John is a cat. Mary is a fish. John knocked the fishbowl over and broke it. Mary dies from lack of water.

Evaluation

NOTES:

SESSION 7

Name Game

Group Discussion

Deadlines make me feel...

Materials

None.

Directions

The counselor announces to the group that they are going to pretend to prepare to make a report for a class assignment.

Solicit ideas from the group as to how to begin and proceed.

The following ideas may be discussed:

1. Make a time line for researching and writing the report.
2. Identify sources of information (books, magazines, reference books, media specialist, parents, etc.).
3. Gather information through skimming and reading for detail.
4. Read chapter headings, sub-headings, and summary.
5. Try to identify major points.
6. Look up words you don't understand.
7. Outline major ideas.
8. Take notes on index cards.
9. Summarize in your own words.

Evaluation

NOTES:

Appendices
A through D

APPENDIX A

<u>PARENTAL PERMISSION LETTER SENT TO ALL PARENTS</u>
<u>AT THE BEGINNING OF THE SCHOOL YEAR</u>

Dear Parents,

As part of our school's developmental guidance program, students are invited to participate in small group counseling sessions. Children who share a common concern meet together with the counselor to talk and share. Membership in the four groups described below is based on parental referral. If, after reading the following descriptions, you feel your child might benefit from participation in any of these groups, please fill out the form below and return it to your child's teacher or the school counselor.

DIVORCE COUNSELING GROUP is for students who are experiencing or who have experienced a divorce in their families. Students are encouraged to ask questions, clarify conflicts, and share feelings regarding divorce. Experience shows that the greatest benefit from this group is the support children feel from each other.

CHILDREN OF ALCOHOLISM GROUP is for students who live with or have close contact with someone who has a drinking problem. Emphasis will be on understanding alcoholism as a disease and learning how to cope with the associated problems as a child.

INCARCERATED FAMILY MEMBERS GROUP is for students who have a family member in jail. Emphasis is on the child's feelings about the situation and coping strategies for dealing with the situation.

DEATH COUNSELING GROUP is for students who have suffered the loss of a loved one or a pet. Emphasis is on understanding the stages of grief and sharing the hurt with others who understand.

Participation in each of these groups will involve weekly meetings during the school day. Our meeting format will include discussion and activities. Students will be expected to respect the confidential nature of our discussions when they return to their classes. If you have any questions about the guidance program, I would welcome the opportunity to discuss them with you.

_____
Counselor

I give my permission for my child, _____, to participate in the following group(s):

_____ Divorce   _____ Alcoholism   _____ Incarceration   _____ Death

_____   _____
Parent's Signature   Teacher

APPENDIX B

SELF-CONCEPT INVENTORY

Circle the appropriate letter.	Always	Sometimes	Never
1. I like myself.	A	S	N
2. I like my family.	A	S	N
3. I like school.	A	S	N
4. I am a good student.	A	S	N
5. I am a good friend.	A	S	N
6. I like to do new things.	A	S	N
7. I like to meet new people.	A	S	N
8. I make new friends easily.	A	S	N
9. I finish what I start to do.	A	S	N
10. I can keep a secret.	A	S	N
11. My parents treat me fairly.	A	S	N
12. My teacher understands me.	A	S	N
13. I am proud of myself.	A	S	N
14. I can do at least one thing well.	A	S	N

Circle the words which describe you right now.

happy	sad	scared	embarrassed
nervous	calm	lucky	angry
annoyed	puzzled	excited	worried
special	hungry	sleepy	patient

APPENDIX C

INCOMPLETE SENTENCES WORK SHEET

1. If I had three wishes, I would wish for:

   _____

   _____

   _____

2. I worry about _____

3. I am good at _____

4. I am afraid of _____

5. I don't like _____

6. If I were principal of this school, I would _____

   _____

7. Something you probably don't know about me is _____

   _____

8. I would like to learn to _____

   _____

9. I would like to visit _____

10. I might want to talk to the school counselor privately about ___

    _____

    _____

    _____

    _____

    _____

APPENDIX D

EVALUATION SHEET FOR GROUP PARTICIPATORS

Please evaluate your group sessions by circling the appropriate answers.

1. Was the time spent in our group sessions worthwhile?	Yes	No
2. Did you learn anything about yourself through participation in this group?	Yes	No
3. Did you learn anything about getting along with others through participation in our group?	Yes	No
4. Given another opportunity, would you choose to participate in another counseling group?	Yes	No
5. Were you satisfied with your counselor's leadership in the group sessions?	Yes	No
6. Did you ever talk to anyone outside of the group about your participation?	Yes	No
7. Have you ever discussed our group with your parents?	Yes	No
8. Did you look forward to our meeting times?	Yes	No
9. Has there been any change in your behavior since participation in our group?	Yes	No

ADDITIONAL COMMENTS

NOTES

NOTES

NOTES

NOTES

NOTES

NOTES

NOTES